THE SMOKING DIARIES

To David

Merry Christmas 06

Merry

from

Santa Sorry

Also by Simon Gray

Non-fiction
AN UNNATURAL PURSUIT AND OTHER PIECES
HOW'S THAT FOR TELLING 'EM, FAT LADY?
FAT CHANCE
ENTER A FOX

Fiction
COLMAIN
SIMPLE PEOPLE
LITTLE PORTIA
A COMEBACK FOR STARK
BREAKING HEARTS

Stage plays
published by Faber and Faber
WISE CHILD, DUTCH UNCLE, THE IDIOT, SPOILED, BUTLEY, OTHERWISE ENGAGED, DOG
DAYS, MOLLY, THE REAR COLUMN, CLOSE OF PLAY, STAGESTRUCK, QUARTERMAINE'S
TERMS, THE COMMON PURSUIT, MELON, HIDDEN LAUGHTER,
THE HOLY TERROR, CELL MATES, SIMPLY DISCONNECTED
published by Nick Hern Books
JUST THE THREE OF US, THE LATE MIDDLE CLASSES, JAPES

Television plays
THE CARAMEL CRISIS, DEATH OF A TEDDY BEAR, A WAY WITH THE LADIES,
SLEEPING DOG, SPOILED, PIG IN A POKE, THE DIRT ON LUCY LANE, THE PRINCESS, MAN IN
A SIDE-CAR, PLAINTIFFS AND DEFENDANTS, TWO SUNDAYS

Radio plays
THE HOLY TERROR, THE RECTOR'S DAUGHTER, SUFFER THE LITTLE CHILDREN,
WITH A NOD AND A BOW

Television films
AFTER PILKINGTON, QUARTERMAINE'S TERMS, OLD FLAMES, THEY NEVER SLEPT,
THE COMMON PURSUIT, RUNNING LATE, UNNATURAL PURSUITS, FEMME FATALE

Films
BUTLEY, A MONTH IN THE COUNTRY

THE
SMOKING
DIARIES

Simon Gray

CARROLL & GRAF PUBLISHERS
NEW YORK

THE SMOKING DIARIES

Carroll & Graf Publishers
An Imprint of Avalon Publishing Group Inc.
245 West 17th Street
New York, NY 10011

AVALON
publishing group incorporated

First published in Great Britain by Granta Books 2004
Copyright © 2004 by Simon Gray

Extract on page 65 from *Enter a Fox* by Simon Gray,
Originally published by Faber and Faber 2001

First Carroll & Graf edition 2005

Library of Congress Cataloging-in-Publication Data is available.

ISBN: 0-7867-1545-6

9 8 7 6 5 3 2 1

Printed in the United States of America
Typset by M Rules
Distributed by Publishers Group West

For Dena

Simon Gray, London, 2002

1

HAPPY BIRTHDAY, SWEETHEART

So here I am, two hours into my sixty-sixth year. From tomorrow on I'm entitled to various benefits, or so I gather – a state pension of so many pounds a week, free travel on public transport, reduced fees on the railways. I assume I'm also entitled to subsidiary benefits – a respectful attention when I speak, unfailing assistance when I stumble or lurch, an absence of registration when I do the things I've been doing more and more frequently recently, but have struggled to keep under wraps – belching, farting, dribbling, wheezing. I can do all these things openly and publicly now, in a spirit of mutual acceptance. Thus am I, at sixty-five and a day. Thus he is, at sixty-five and a day, a farter, a belcher, a dribbler and a what else did I say I did, farting, belching, dribbling, oh yes, wheezing. But then as I smoke something like sixty-five cigarettes a day people are likely to continue with their inevitable 'Well, if you insist on getting through three packets, etc.' to which I will reply, as always – actually, I can't remember what I always reply, and how could I, when I don't believe anyone, even my doctors, ever says anything like, 'Well, if you will insist, etc.' In fact, I'm merely reporting a conversation I have with myself, quite often, when I find myself wheezing my way not only up but down the stairs, and when I recover from dizzy spells after pulling on my socks, tying up my shoelaces, two very distinct acts. No, four very distinct acts, each separated by an interval longer than the acts themselves. Naturally, like most people of sixty-five and a day I only grasp my age, the astonishing number of years I've completed, by these physical symptoms – within, the child, about eight years old, rages away – I wish it were all reversed, that I had the appetites, physical stamina, and desirability of a healthy eight-year-old, and the inner life of a man of sixty-five and a day as I imagine it to be from the point of view of an eight-year-old – calm, beneficent, worldly-wise and brimming with tolerance, not to mention forgiveness, yes, I need to be in touch with my inner adult, is the truth of the matter, who has always been lost to me except as an idea. But the truth is that I'm nastier than I used to be back when – back when I was sixty-four, for instance, when I was nastier than I was at sixty-two and so forth, back and back, always the less nasty the further back, until I get to the age when I was pre-nasty, at least consciously, when the only shame I knew was the shame of being found out which was when I was, well, about eight, I suppose.

TWO FRIENDS IN A PLIGHT

What's the date? Well, it's Friday midnight the week before Christmas, and this is what happened this evening – at about the time when Victoria and I were vaguely preparing to cross the road to dinner at Chez Moi, there was a ring on the doorbell. We froze, she in her study, I in mine, waiting for the bell to ring again or for the bell ringer to go away – we have a policy, since we were mugged on the pavement outside the house, never to answer the door in the evening unless we know for certain who's there. The bell didn't ring again. 'Any idea who that might have been?' I bellowed huskily (pretty exact description – my voice, when used normally, is low and broken from fifty-seven years of smoking but when raised it comes out husky), 'Did you get a look?' – sometimes she pops into the bedroom when the doorbell rings, and peeks down from the window – no, she said, she'd seen a shape at the frosted glass in the front door, but couldn't tell anything, not even the sex, it had only been a glimpse, really, from the top of the stairs. 'Well,' I said, 'did you get a sense? Did you hear the footsteps? Could it have been a policeman?' I have a dread of policemen at the door, bearing bad news, a hangover from the years when my children were at that sort of stage – Lucy's first car, Ben's tendency to stray into unprotected areas, unprotected from himself, in some cases – yes, it could have been a policeman, Victoria said, but then it could have been anyone, as she hadn't heard anything, but I was suddenly convinced that I had, that I'd heard the heavy tread, with something slow and deliberate in it, of a policeman, though now I come to think of it, it would have to have been a policeman from another age, a policeman from *Dixon of Dock Green*, if not Dixon himself, the policemen of these days don't have a heavy tread, for one thing they don't wear constabulary boots, they wear light, smart shoes that probably cause them to pitter-patter lightly along, in twos or threes or even little packs of four or five, towards some pop star whose Internet habit they are investigating – clearly, then, if I'd thought about it, the heavy tread I hadn't heard hadn't belonged to a policeman, but not having thought about it and now actually assuming our bell had been rung by a policeman, actually picturing him in his helmet, heavy jacket, enveloping blue trousers, and his large boots, we crossed the road to Chez Moi and saw, as we entered, the Pinters, Harold and Antonia seated at a table facing the door, in the second room.

'I came across a moment ago, and rang your bell, to see if you wanted to join us,' Antonia said. 'I saw somebody through the glass at the top of the stairs, so I knew you were in.' We reminded her of our policy of never answering the door until we know who is at it, without of course explaining that I'd mistaken her tread, which I hadn't actually heard, for that of a policeman from a distant epoch, but it struck me as unusual, not to say unprecedented, for her to have rung the doorbell, and there was something in Harold's manner, subdued and soft in his greetings –

'The thing is,' he said, almost as soon as we'd sat down, 'I might as well tell you, I've just discovered – well, today in fact, that I've got cancer.'

The world went immediately upside down and into a spin. In all the years, etc., the standing order of things is that I'm the one that gets ill, hovers now and then at death's door, and he is the robust one, seeming almost to get more robust with the passing of time – furthermore it's always been a condition, an absolute condition, of my relationship with him, as I've understood it, that he should still be in the world when I leave it, just as he was when I entered it.

He went through the stages of the treatment that lay ahead for him – that he would begin it two days after Christmas, then there would be a break of three weeks during which the poisons would be at their business of attacking the cancer, then another all-day session followed by another three weeks, by which time there would be, he noted matter of factly, certain physical changes, his face might alter in shape, his hair might fall out – 'But of course you know the procedure,' he said to me, 'from Ian. How's he doing?'

'Not too well,' I said, and gave him the information Ian had given to me, just last night as a matter of fact, and also in Chez Moi, at a table around the corner from the one we were now sitting at – I tried to be crisp and impersonal, and stopped myself saying, 'But of course his isn't anything like yours, his is far worse' – which would be true inasmuch as I understand the matter, Harold's cancer being local, in his oesophagus, Ian's being all over the place, in his liver, his lungs, probably now also in his lymph – but I didn't think he'd want me to offer consolation by stressing the direness of Ian's plight – direness of Ian's plight! Christ! What a phrase – I've never used it before in my life, where did it come from, direness, plight, when I mean that actually I think he's dying.

How will Harold manage?

He'll manage well, I think. With endurance, resolution. Grit. He has a lot of that, thank God.

ON HOLIDAY

I talked to Rollocks for a short while, about the moon, which was three quarters full, or a quarter empty, depending on your temperament, and then we talked about cricket, the tragic decline of West Indies cricket, then what it is like to find ourselves in the computer age. Rollocks is perhaps five years younger than me, but older in terms of dignity, bearing, manner of speech. He brought me a specially chilled diet coke. The bar is empty, apart from Rollocks, who never presides over any customer but myself, as far as I can make out. His hours begin at 11 p.m. and end at 7 a.m., and his function is to provide all-night service to a clientele who tend to be in bed as he arrives on the premises, and to be about to rise as he leaves them. I can't say that the clientele is all elderly – quite a few are much younger than me, but they seem to settle into elderly habits, early days, early nights. I don't imagine that they even notice that everyone else does as they do, or that they do as everyone else does, but often, when I walk around the grounds at half-past midnight, I find every light in the apartments and cottages is out, and the hotel takes on the aspect of a large nest, humming with sleep – and then later there are Rollocks and I in the bar, where we too follow a pattern – a short conversation, he brings the diet coke, I write. Last night I wrote a letter to Harold. I don't remember now quite what I said – I know I mentioned Rollocks, and then went into a little bit about the hotel and I wrote about the weather, and the mosquitoes, all of this uneasily, as I was trying to find my way towards the central issue, the state of Harold's health – wondering how the treatment was going, how his appetite was, whether his temperature had dropped, etc. – and from there I went into my own feelings when I'd been ill to the point of death five years ago, that I'd found it unbearable to be with people because they seemed to me to be coming from another country, or rather that I'd been exiled to another country and they were paying me brief, troubled visits, then back they went to where I'd once belonged – and then I found myself refining – or possibly coarsening – this thought by adding that actually I'd felt I was under arrest for a rather sad crime, that in some sense the exile was, or seemed to be, a moral one. I'm not sure that this was an appropriate line to take – how can it be helpful to a man perhaps mortally afflicted to have it suggested that he might actually be in the throes of committing some social offence? Well, I've already posted the letter – I know I've posted it, so why did I suddenly start looking for it – I actually picked up my hat as if the letter to Harold I know I've posted might nevertheless be under it. Why did I bring the hat down anyway? It's a straw hat, I wear it to keep the sun off my head, and although I'm outside, it's two in the morning, no sun, just a quarter moon, as I believe I've already –

So a little pause, to light a cigarette, a sip of diet coke, calm restored. I've put the hat on my head – Ian's hat actually, that he wore to cover the effects of chemotherapy and has been passed on to me – not quite true that I claimed a few days after his death. When I was told that he'd wanted me to have something, he probably meant from his library, but I immediately asked for his hat, on which I keep far too attentive an eye, clasping at it when it's windy, fearful I might forget it when I've taken it off on the beach, now wearing it at night in the bar. I'll have to get over this, I'm bound to lose it, it's in the nature of straw hats to detach themselves from you eventually, much better to accept its loss now and adopt a more sensibly careless attitude to it, thinking that I can always get a new one. Of course, the thing about Ian is – no, I can't remember him, not at the moment, his expressions, voice, etc., all I can remember is his coffin being carried down the aisle, then being loaded onto the hearse. He was quite a tall man, as tall as me, and the coffin looked too small – but then that's often the way with coffins, miracles of packaging, a body with all those knobs and joints and so forth packed away. Well, his hat is on my head. I'll try to hang on to it.

GOOD MORNING

I had to get up at 6.30 this morning for a pee – on the way back to bed I popped on to the terrace for a quick gander at the breaking dawn which, as it turned out, wasn't breaking, the light was grey, and the pale trees and the shrubbery shifting about irritably in a sharp wind, the only signs of human life a strange and stooped figure on the beach, moving spectrally between a couple of beach-beds under one of the charmingly shaped (like a coolie's hat) straw and wooden-poled little edifices that provide a circle of shade only a few feet from the sea – there are only three of these shelters, which

are not only delightful to look at but delightful to be under – a
small shelf for drinks encircles the pole, altogether a home from
home – and they are much prized and competed for – now the
rules of the hotel, I should explain, regarding beach-beds, chairs,
etc. are really quite simple, indeed there is only one clear rule, when
it comes down to it – first come, first served, but on a day-to-day
basis, in other words you can't keep your cherished location for the
length of your stay, you have to establish your claim to it every
morning – thus the spectre in the 6.20 a.m. gloom – he was staking
his claim for the day, though he seemed to be doing rather more
than that, stooping now over this bed, now over that, kneeling at
the table on the pole, bowing to the sea – he was wearing the hotel
dressing gown, a short number with greyish blue and white stripes,
institutional, a prison or hospital sort of thing that nevertheless in
the context conferred on him a sort of authority, and made it seem
as if he were performing a ceremony of a ritualistic nature, a
blessing perhaps – I peered closer and realized that he was elderly,
older than me even, and by quite a bit, and that what he was doing
was elderly business, exactly the sort of thing that I've been doing
for a few years now – and it gets worse and worse – when I try to
sort myself out somewhere, picking things up, putting them down
in order to pick something else up for reasons unknown, putting
it down, stopping to work out a puzzle to do with, for instance, the
whereabouts of a towel that one had thought one had adjusted a
moment ago, but now seems to have vanished from the scene of the
action, on and on it goes, fiddling, fussing, farting around – and
superstition comes into it somewhere, the fear that if one hasn't got
every detail – as when he kept edging a bed inches sideways from
one end, going to the other end and inching it back again, pushing
it forwards, pulling it backwards, standing to inspect it, making a
further adjustment – was this one for his wife, slumbering in their

room, unaware that her husband was fretting and fiddling at inches and angles for her sake, would she even notice when she came to the beach the exact arrangement of her bed, and how could she notice, really, as there was nothing specific for it to be exact to, unless of course she'd provided him with exact instructions – my bed is to be precisely at such an angle to the sea/sun when we come down at 8 a.m. sort of stuff, no, these impulses were coming from *within* him, and mine come from within me, synapses or whatever they are that control these matters, going into a muddled repeat mode, doing almost the same thing again and again, the deep-laid purpose, if there is one, is never to finish the inessential task – no, that's not true, getting out of the house is sometimes essential, when I have to meet people or go to the dentist across the street, but getting out of the house – making it from my study to the pavement without going back for something it turns out I haven't forgotten can take ten to fifteen minutes, which I fill by performing inessential tasks again and again – put my spare spectacles in the case for safety's sake, take them out again straight away for future convenience's sake, decide to swap spare spectacles for the ones I'm using, decide to swap the spare spectacles I'm not using for the ones I've just made spare – I become increasingly desperate during all this, crying out, 'What am I doing? Why am I doing this?' generally culminating in a scream, a husky scream, because of my smoking, 'God, I hate myself!' So I found myself hating the old guy who seemed really to be doing a studied and detailed imitation of me. I watched him walk a few steps away from the benches, stop, turn, crouch clutching his knees (I can't do this . . . joints too stiff), peer at the bench, then back for some more rearranging, then away only a few paces this time, and back, at it again. Finally, he made it to the path above the beach that will take him back to his snoozing wife – or mistress, young, vibrant, preparing herself for a pre-breakfast frolic, while her man – 'my man' – is out there, not hunting/gathering, but fiddling and faddling for her sake – perhaps the realigning was really to give himself angles from which he can peer between her legs or down into her breasts. But I don't think so. Nothing of the eager scamper, the driven scuttle, in the way he groped his way through the greyness, across the lawns towards his room – or somebody else's room, his legs looked as if they didn't care much where they took him, as long as it was somewhere very close. As he tottered around the palm trees and out of sight, I had an impulse to zip – a word I like to use for my own totter – down the stairs, across the lawn to his nest, snatch up his towels, zip back up here, thus providing Victoria and myself with four towels instead of the usual two, and further providing somebody else with the opportunity of marking out the most desired spot on the beach, and further providing the possibility of the most magnificent row after breakfast when he and his wife come to loll in their rightful place, and find two others, I'd hope of the same age, but of different nationalities, two elderly French versus two middle-aged Scots would be best, but really I would accept any combination – the impulse didn't pass. I took it to bed with me, and nourished it a while as I lay with my arms wrapped around my wife, who was deeply asleep and mumbling slightly. Now that I've written this, I'll spend the rest of the day reading. I feel a strong need for what in my Cambridge days, my Leavis days, was considered a life-enhancing book, though I'm not sure what sort of book a life-enhancing book would be, when it comes to it. Or even what enhancing means when connected to a book. I suppose it must have spiritual implications. The only writer who actually changed my life for the better in any practical and measurable way was Hank Janson, who gave me what I had for a sex life when I was twelve years old – at that age I had no idea of what was to be found between a girl's legs, but partly assumed, mystically assumed, it would be a prettier, daintier, more feminine version of what was to be found between my own, and I couldn't imagine, of course, how they could interact, hers and mine. So Hank Janson – the titles alone drove my blood wild – *Torment for Trixy* – *Hotsy, You'll Be Chilled* – and on the cover a vivid blonde, blouse ripped, skirt hitched up to her thighs, struggling sweetly against chains, ropes, a gag – and in the top right corner set in a small circle, like a medallion, the silhouette of presumably Hank himself, trench coat open, trilby tilted back, a cigarette hanging from a corner of his mouth.

UNDER THE INFLUENCES

His real name was Frances Stephen or Stephen Frances, one or the other surfaced in the newspapers when he was on the run in – when would that have been, roughly? the year Hank Janson was on the run, well, it was when I was fifteen or so, and as I was born in 1936, 1936 + 15 = 1951. Yes, that's about right, 1951. Now what the thing was about Hank Janson was that he was –

Start again. Hank Janson.

I kept my Hank Janson library squirrelled away in different nooks and crannies of my bedroom, some under a loose floorboard, and as an extra security measure, I tore the covers off and concealed them between the pages of the books, so I naturally assumed that this secret cache was entirely unknown to my mother, who never mentioned that she knew about it except once, obliquely. She came into the dining room where my brother Nigel and I had just started our breakfast – a meal my mother cooked before dressing for the day – generally she wore a flapping dressing gown over an almost transparent nightie, so I suppose, on reflection, I could have found out what was to be found, or rather not to be found, between a girl's legs by dropping to my knees – but of course both Nigel and I kept our eyes averted, from each other as well as from her, as she flung herself into and out of the dining room talking constantly and comically or reproachfully, pausing to gesture with her cigarette, laughing at something she'd said –

Now the thing about Mummy, Mummy and me, well, actually it was I whom she frankly –

Frankly, I was the one she loved to fondle, the one she made sit on her lap, whose legs she stroked, whose hair she ruffled, the nape of whose neck she kissed, etc., and so forth, while Nigel and his father (well, our father, but I tended to see them as a twosome) stood or sat by with the appearance of disdain for all these displays of full-blooded passion – yes, that was it – Mummy and I were the adoring couple, Nigel and Daddy were a pair of disapproving relatives – great-uncle and uncle perhaps, though that doesn't work out – oh yes, it does if you see Daddy as Mummy's uncle, and Nigel as mine, everything slots into place, anthropologically speaking – is anthropology the right science for these delicate matters, or should we be thinking of psychiatry here – well, these days, of course, one should be thinking of column inches in the *Mail on Sunday*, with myself portrayed as Mummy's toy boy, and Nigel and Daddy as the jilted lovers bonding. There is one memory, though, that abruptly and discordantly intrudes itself into the family idyll. There I was, hunched on the lavatory, brooding over my latest Hank Janson, when the door burst open, and there was my father.

'Get out,' I ordered, speaking from a self I didn't know I owned.

'Sorry,' said my father, and got out . . .

When I eventually came out of the bathroom on to the landing, I could hear their voices from the bedroom, he was talking quietly, with brio, a lively mutter, not his usual tone or style at all, and she was gasping with suppressed laughter – the obvious effort to maintain low audibility being from tact, I like to think, although they both knew the acoustics of the house well enough to know what carried where. I don't know exactly what I anticipated – scenes, showdowns, confiscations certainly, worst of all a long morbid conversation, anyway not parental laughter, my doting Mummy laughing at her wanking (this word didn't exist at the time, at least in my circles) son, so I was at first mortified, then relieved, then mortified again but in a – not comfortable, of course not, but – but secure sort of way. Loved. I can't remember how I sidled into view at breakfast time, so I assume it was as usual, Mummy's long legs scissoring her in and out of the dining room – Daddy didn't have breakfast with us, he had it in bed – this was the marital routine, Mummy down at seven to make a cup of tea, take it up to Daddy with the newspapers and the post, then she'd slip back into bed, then downstairs to make our breakfast, then in term time Nigel and I off to school, he to St Paul's, I to Westminster, and Daddy, shortly afterwards, off to the Belgrave Hospital, near the Oval, where he was the pathologist. We lived in Oakley Gardens, Chelsea, now a swank address, but then a slummy, no, not slummy, a down-at-heel professional classes neighbourhood at a time when the professional classes, particularly doctors, were overtaxed and underpaid, and my father, for instance, hard pressed to pay our school fees. England of half a century ago, depleted by war, only just emerging from rationing, restricted in travel (sixty pounds per annum per adult), long orderly queues on the pavements outside the butcher's, the fishmonger's, the sweet shops, I could go on listing the deprivations of this victorious nation, because they were all around us, affecting every aspect of our lives, but of course they were, for Nigel and myself and all those of our age and younger, the natural conditions of life, as were the daily civilities – the calm, the sense of safety. There was a working-class estate, the Peabody Buildings, directly behind the small backyards of the houses along our side of Oakley Gardens, and there was Chelsea Manor Street with its 'bombed outs' living on council estates, and a small cluster of prefabs at one end – so a continuous if accidental mingling of classes, but I never once, in the seven years we lived there, heard an obscenity on the street, let alone saw a violent gesture, though occasionally, when going up Chelsea Manor Street to swim in the public baths, Nigel and I would be encircled at an unintimidating distance by a group rather than a gang of working-class boys of our age or older, and jeered at for being posh – and that was it, the class war, as experienced by the two Gray brothers half a century ago, when there really were visibly defined classes, working/lower, lower-middle, middle, upper-middle, and upper . . . but enough history, enough sociology, back to 47 Oakley Gardens, sometime in 1951, to the breakfast that followed my mortification on the lavatory, Daddy upstairs in bed with his tea, post and papers, Mummy now downstairs, flying about in her transparent nightie, cigarette hanging from the side of her mouth – but no, that's not the breakfast I'm after, it's a subsequent breakfast, some weeks or possibly even months later. She stalked into the dining room, head held high – an ominous sign – in her hands a plate for Nigel, a plate for me, she flung the plates down with a flourish, drew on her cigarette with a flourish, released a long cloud of smoke. 'That filthy man Hank Janson has run away,' she said. 'Did you know that?'

Impossible to describe the effect of those two words – Hank and Janson – coming from her lips. It was mysterious, omniscient, terrifying. How did she know? How? In retrospect, I can see that Mummy being my mother, and having heard from father Daddy about the presence of the book (he couldn't have seen the cover, given my posture) over which I'd been bent, with warm wings brooding, as the Jesuit poet, Gerard Manley Hopkins, once described his own solitary labourings – no, no, it was God in the poem, God who did the brooding, with warm wings, ah, my dear! Nothing to do with my sort of brooding at all, although some critics have hinted that the strain of Hopkins's celibacy might have given rise to the explosive, ejaculatory nature of his verse – now what was I? Oh, yes, Mummy and her 'That filthy man Hank Janson has run away!'

'Where to?' Nigel said at last, thus seeming to demonstrate not simply a lack of surprise, but the possibility of a vast reservoir of knowledge – at the very least of some of the circumstances that would have caused Hank to run.

'He's wanted for writing lewd and disgusting and obscene books,' our mother replied, at an angle to Nigel's question, 'wanted by the police.' And by me, too, for the same thing. She jabbed her cigarette at us, and left us to it.

There followed a brief squabble as to whose hoard she'd unearthed. 'Not mine,' said Nigel confidently, 'I've only got one, and it's behind the wardrobe, I've pushed it so far back I can hardly get at it myself.' He'd done this on purpose, he explained, because he was trying to give up Hank Janson because he was trying to get into the St Paul's rugger colts, and because he was preparing to take Communion. 'Well, it's not me,' I said, although it obviously was, my Jansons squirrelled into so many corners that Mother would have needed little inspiration to turn up one of them within a minute or so, once she'd decided to search – or perhaps she always did a search, a routine search, but didn't grasp the significance of what she turned up until her husband reported to her what he'd observed of their son on the lavatory, and the *Daily Mail* reported to her that the writer Janson was on the run – these days, of course, he would have been protected by Index on Censorship, PEN, Amnesty International, Writers in Prison.

In fact, he made it to Spain. I know this because I sat next to his agent – he'd been my agent too, for a brief period – on a London bus one afternoon, about thirty-five years ago. I can't imagine the context in which Janson's name came up, we certainly didn't know each other well enough to trade information about our youthful sexual habits – anyway he told me that Janson had fled to Spain, where he had written novels about the Spanish civil war which always contained one scene of bondage, not of the former playful, fanciful kind, in which there was merely male dominance over sweetly rebellious femininity – the Spanish bondage was gritty, nasty, cruel – political, in other words – heroic Republican guerrillas, female rather than feminine (beautiful nonetheless), brutalized by Franco's thugs, beaten, raped, murdered – he (the agent) had been astonished by the change in tone and style, but the thing was, he said, that the passion in the politics was quite genuine – these novels, which he'd written under his real name – Stephen Francis or Francis Stephens – were serious works, properly researched and constructed, bits of dialogue in Spanish. One or two – I think he mentioned a trilogy – had been published in hardback. He still lived in Spain, prospered there in fact – it was where he'd always wanted to go, just as he'd always wanted to write the novels he was now writing, so actually he was grateful for his enforced exile, grateful that he'd been hounded out of the dark little office in Soho where he'd dictated the saucy and ebullient works of his early phase to a middle-aged woman who was now his wife – no, I don't believe this last bit, I've added it on to my memory of the conversation – why? – but that his amanuensis was middle-aged, yes, that makes perfect sense, I can accept that, though it's far more entrancing to think that she was in her twenties, sitting with her legs crossed, skirt hitched, stocking top visible, a blonde curl tumbling over her forehead, bent over her pad as her pen flies across the page – and Hank, his feet propped on his desk, hat tilted to the back of his head, cigarette hanging from the corner of his mouth (like Mummy), rapping out his sentences – 'fought like a wild cat' – 'her arms up behind her back' – 'bound them tightly together with the stockings I'd unclipped from her suspenders' – 'lay there on the floor, panting, eyes flashing fury' – 'stared down at the two softly heaving mounds' – 'gentle slopes of' – 'as she opened her mouth to scream I' – 'fastened it behind her neck with my –' he was a small man, the agent said, with crinkly brown hair, and I'll bet he married his secretary, whether the agent told me he did or not, and they live in a grand little villa outside Malaga, perhaps – I'm glad he came out on the Republican side, though the handcuffs aspect of his writing seems more falangist – but really there is probably little connection between a man's sexual obsessions and his political inclinations – think of Kenneth Tynan, a theatre critic of the sixties and seventies (twentieth century), a prominent supporter of all left-wing and libertarian causes, who devoted the last decade of his life to spanking women, thinking about spanking women, brooding endlessly about spanking women – but perhaps that is libertarian, though probably not left-wing, because whatever you think about spanking women –

– a few yards from where I'm sitting, writing this, is

AN UNTROUBLED MIND

a very fine-looking, stiff-backed old gentleman, with fine white hair and a calm and steady gaze. His smile is cryptic and serene. He is holding a magazine, which he now and then consults, but mainly his gaze is fixed ahead, making it seem not only calm and steady, but inward-looking, as if his past were some vast landscape that he can keep unfolded, his to survey and command. His wife is possibly younger than he, perhaps a decade younger, but then his stillness and nobly contemplative air make him seem ageless, while she looks as if she's been at the same age for most of her life – perhaps since she met him, took control of all the trivial problems of his days and nights – she's stout, stubby – yes, a little stub of a woman, with a small, ugly, determined face, hair cut brutishly short, her eyes bulging slightly, her brow dark and heavy – not exactly angry, rather furiously anxious – she has dreadful varicose veins, knobs of them on her calves, she stumps about in flip-flops, baggy shorts, tending to her seraphic husband, bringing him plastic cups of water, removing the magazine as soon as he loses interest in it, which is almost immediately, putting it back in his hands, helping him out of his chair and into another chair – tending, tending, furiously and anxiously tending, occasionally talking to him in abrupt sentences, sometimes with a whiny tone, sometimes eagerly, pointing out, for instance, that the hotel isn't a hotel, it's composed of small chalets, each one containing a bedroom and a bathroom and a balcony – he gives her a condescending and rather empty attention while she utters these imbecilities – after all, they are inhabiting one of the chalets themselves, and the one they inhabit must look pretty much like all the other chalets, how dare she disturb this distinguished consciousness to so little purpose, is the thought that goes through one's mind as off she goes, to find him an unwanted towel, or take his walking stick from the back of the chair, propping it beside him or putting it between his legs so that his hands can fold around its top – and then once or twice she presses affection on him – Victoria reports that she saw her once bend suddenly, while she was fiddling about his person, and kiss him full on the lips, then fiddle a bit more before kissing him fully on the lips again – this from a little dog of a stumpy woman to a man contemplating the eternities within – once I saw her take him by the hand and lead him gently to the edge of the lawn, then down the path that leads to the opening to the beach, then several yards across the sand, the two of them toddling hand in hand, it was most poignant, the childlikeness of it. I've just glanced over his shoulder as I passed (deliberately, I must admit) behind him and saw the cover of the magazine that he was holding passively in his lap. It's called *Bravo Spain*, and is evidently a travel/tourist publication, clearly without meaning to him, and it occurs to me that he has Alzheimer's, or one of its variants, and that all her dogged, furious tending, her changes of tone and sudden open and passionate and tender displays of affection are attempts to compensate externally for all he has lost, and no doubt is still losing within – how hopeless it all is, really, there's no getting away from it when one sees such things – the things people do to the very end and then past the very end – and, you know, I can't imagine them married, or young, or in middle age or even the year or so back when he started to go, and when I try, the question persists unworthily, 'Whatever did he see in her?' to which she provides the answer in virtually every one of her actions – if I look elsewhere there is affection to be seen among the many elderly couples in this hotel, hand-holding, caressing, and at night dancing to the unmusical bands and groups – a different one for each night of the week. – it's half past one in the morning, I am at my table, Rollocks is laying the breakfast tables, the sea growls and rustles a few yards away, and I wonder how Harold is. There was a piece in the paper this morning – Saturday – we get the papers here a day late, so it was Friday's *Times* or *Telegraph*, announcing that Harold had cancer of the oesophagus, and then giving a brief account of his life and achievements that read as if it were a compressed combination of a promotional release and an obituary – ghastly to come across it, even though I'd been warned by someone who phoned from London yesterday – I'm not going to write tonight, I shall sit here sipping my diet coke, smoke a cigarette, listen to the sea. First I shall write down one word at the beginning of the next line on my yellow pad, and start from there tomorrow. The word I shall write is –

BOOKS

Oh, yes. So books. What books? I left London in such disarray that I couldn't believe we'd get to the airport, let alone to Barbados – when it came to packing books I flung what was nearest to hand on to the bed for Victoria to pack, and then, of course, when she was unpacking them and I saw from our balcony all those ideal spots for reading – on the lawns, on the beach, in the bar where I'm writing this, on the balcony itself – well, there's a biography of Cardinal Richelieu, the only book I brought with some deliberation. I picked it up with pleasure until I twigged that I didn't want it at all, the book I'd chosen with a degree of consideration was the wrong book, I'm not in the slightest bit interested in Cardinal Richelieu (well, I am – but only the slightest bit), the chap I'm keenly interested in is Talleyrand, now and then Bishop Talleyrand, who began his political career by taking holy orders, receiving Voltaire's blessing almost simultaneously, and went on to survive the catastrophes of France, in fact could be found near the centre of the catastrophes of France from the end of the Ancien Régime through the revolution, through the

Empire, then through the Restoration, then through the Republic – he should have been executed once or twice every decade – 'a shit in silk breeches,' Napoleon called him, perfectly accurately, it seems to me, but Napoleon ended up on St Helena, in the custody of a mean-spirited (or strait-laced, depending on your point of view) English civil servant while old Talleyrand was around to welcome Louis XVIII, Napoleon III, how did he do it, is what I want to know, how did he get away with it, playing with fire almost all his life, burning everybody but himself? Now this is a pathetic account of Talleyrand's life, everything I know about him has gone into a fog, which the book on him would have dispelled if I'd brought it, rather than the book on Richelieu, about whom I'm content to remain in a fog – in fact, apart from a general outline of his life, much muddled by my having seen four or five film versions of *The Three Musketeers*, about the only hard fact I remember is that he suffered from piles, towards the end of his life could scarcely rise from his bed, and when compelled to do so by reasons of state, would have to be carried. There is a very important book – that's what we say these days when wishing to draw attention to what we believe to be a good film, book, play, exhibition, we say that it's 'important', as, for instance, an 'important' new play by so and so (me, for instance), we usually say it in an important manner, our voices becoming grave, heavy, episcopal, so what exactly do I mean when I write that there is a very 'important' book about piles waiting to be written – I think I mean that piles might be found to have affected the course of history now and then – no doubt Richelieu, given his steely mind, his patience and his ambition, would have made the decisions he made if he'd been piles-free, but Napoleon at Borodino, a few hours before the battle which led on to the disaster of Moscow, lingering in his tent, hoping his piles would quieten down so that he could be out and about on his horse, which he couldn't bear to mount – you see how one could go on from there – for want of an ointment – there's one currently on the market called Anus-oil, or very nearly that, which is quite soothing, I believe – for want of a tube of Anus-oil the battle of Borodino was lost – drawn, actually, I think, but a strength-sapping draw, and so the unplanned diversion to Moscow – the rest is history. Yup. Now to move with piles into a different field, take Gary Cooper in *High Noon*, a film recognized as a complete turkey when it opened for try-out showings in the Midwest, audiences laughing, jeering, walking out as jaunty, heroic, sunny even, Gary Cooper strode down the streets of his little town, a parody of the classic Western sheriff – the reason he looked so implausible, however, was that all through the shooting he'd been crippled by piles – every step a torment, which he'd tried to disguise by assuming a bogus jauntiness whenever he could manage it – generally he could do one take in this mode, and that was the take the director felt obliged to use. Well, after the first try-out showings, and the public's response, the producers were in despair, should they can the whole affair and leave Gary Cooper to dwindle into the Hollywood twilight, another star who'd ended in a feeble and melancholy twinkling down? They repaired to the editing room to see if they could find any scenes that actually worked, hoping to build from there, useless, useless, all they had was Gary's piles-driven gait, simultaneously cramped and bow-legged, his face grimacing in agony, his eyes tortured – until somebody – either the director or the editor, though I suppose it might have been the producer – suddenly saw that in the problem lay the solution. They spliced all the scenes in which Gary's piles were at their most inflamed, and looked at what they'd got – the nobly tortured, stoically enduring sheriff that marked a significant if not actually an important turning point in the history of the Western – downhill, in my view, being the only person I know who found the film phoney and inflated on my first viewing and before I knew the facts, but my opinion is neither here nor there in this account, which is concerned with pointing out the crucial part played by piles in the transformation of the film from out-of-town turkey to an Oscars-all-round triumph, with a treasured place – allotted to it by the usual collection of people I'm inclined by nature to disagree with – in the history of the cinema, etc. – though it should be added that further acknowledgement must be made to the magical powers of the editing room, where they added the magnificent theme song sung by Tex Ritter, and the shots of the ticking clock – you can see that it's just been stuck in, the clock, because it's completely bald, so to speak, no human form comes near it, no shadow falls upon it, we just cut to it whenever the director needs to jack up the tension – but mainly the success of the film has to be attributed to Gary's piles, just as Napoleon's failure in Russia has to be attributed to piles – and there are many other stories to be unearthed, I truly believe – what about Coleridge's piles, for instance – discover if there's a connection between the piles, the laudanum and the great hallucinatory poems, 'Ancient Mariner', 'Kubla Khan' – the laudanum, taken to escape the pain from piles, giving him the hallucinations that inspired the poems – was the man from Porlock his dealer, possibly, come to report that his supply had run out, so no more inspiration, no more Kubla. I could go on in this vein –

Oh. I've just come back from a swim – as I was cavorting towards shore, doing my very favourite thing in life, rolling myself underwater, down and down, then bobbing up again, then lolling on my side for a while before dipping back down – I have many of the instincts, though none of the grace, of a porpoise, I believe – I saw a kindred spirit, a recumbent porpoise, toes turned up, arms stretched out, head cushioned on the water. It was the wife of the man with Alzheimer's, the Alzheimer widow, as I've come to think of her, not fussing and worrying and scowling, but taking her ease in the ocean, lolling to the manner born – she got out, quite a difficult manoeuvre on this beach, as there is a steep shelf, and the waves can tumble you about, mixing you into a rush of pebbles and sharp little rocks – but her sturdy, varicosed legs carried her up over the shelf onto the shore, where she picked up a stone, took aim, I thought at first at me, but she swung it well away, across an unpeopled patch of water, with accuracy and skill – it skipped and skipped, it must have done four long skips, then a sequence of shorter ones before going under. She watched it do this with close attention, then turned, and stumped off up the beach. The little incident gave me great pleasure, even more when I passed her a few minutes later, her damp head pressed on Mr Alzheimer's chest. He gazed smiling over her head, benignly unresponsive – then she set about sorting him out, pushing his sunglasses further up his nose, exchanging his magazine for a book, getting him a cup of water –

AUDEN BY MOONLIGHT

Almost the worst part of my book-packing was that I hadn't brought any poetry at all – apart from Ian's, that is, but Ian's is for another kind of reading, to do with him as much as his poems – Wordsworth and Hardy are the two poets I've especially wanted to read, and some Keats, I had a yearning for Keats and also Pope – so I phoned a friend in New York, and asked her to send an anthology, any anthology really that you can lay your hands on quickly, I said, it's really quite urgent, and this is what she sent – the *Oxford Book of English Verse*, edited by Christopher Ricks, which could hardly fail to serve the purpose, and which I now have before me on the table in the bar, and into which I have been dipping and delving for some hours – the last hour with some difficulty, as the electricity suddenly cut off, as it does from time to time in Barbados, and I've had to read by the light of the moon (a mere sliver), two candles, and an oil lamp, all furnished by Rollocks – well, the moon-sliver wasn't furnished by Rollocks, of course, he provided just the candles and the lamp, and frankly they didn't produce much in the way of illumination, more a smoky pool that drew to it moths and mosquitoes and other rubbish on wings, but I was so in need of poetry that I'd probably have made do with my lighter, and the glow from my cigarette – I started with Ricks's Preface and Introduction – I scarcely ever read prefaces and introductions to anthologies of poetry, assuming that the collection will make its own argument, no need to apologize or explain, here they are, these poems as opposed to those poems, have a good time – but this time – it was when we still had the electricity – I settled down to both, really settled, clamped on my glasses, lit a cigarette, put my elbow on the table, my left thumb on my left cheek – my en garde position for serious reading – and read. The preface was a two-minute job, but the introduction was the real thing, full of zing and zest, chirrupy, affable and informative, occasionally sinister into the bargain – he tells us to admire Matthew Arnold for the way he 'made friends with the necessity of death' for example, which reminded me of that chap in Muswell Hill, or was it Crouch End, who kept the bodies of his victims in his armchairs, and some of their heads in the fridge – Nielsen, I think the name was – Ricks seems to have

been around as long as I have, reviewing here, there and
everywhere, Professor of English here (Cambridge), there (Oxford)
and everywhere (Harvard, Yale, Princeton etc.) – if I ever run into
him I'll tell him how much I like his selection, I've already come
across lots of things I'm either not familiar with, or had
forgotten – the Hardy is very good, and the Keats, but then there
are a couple of poems at the end, by contemporaries, that are –
well, they're not terrible, exactly, not in themselves, but in the
company they're keeping they seem unworthy, well, worthless in
fact – friends of Ricks, perhaps? but on the other hand there's less
Auden than usual, even if there's still too much, but then any
Auden is too much, as far as I'm concerned – in fact it was while
I was scowling down at 'Musée des Beaux Arts' that the lights went
out, as if the hotel generator were connected to my consciousness,
which also went out as soon as it encountered the first line – I used
to nag away at Ian about it, 'About suffering they were never
wrong, the Old Masters' – how can you be right or wrong about
suffering? And as for 'the Old Masters' – well, the old masters,
whoever they were, were young, or anyway alive when they
painted their paintings, they weren't being old masters, or masters
of anything except the palette to hand, the canvas in front of
them – so I would nag away at Ian, hey, what about the horse at
the end, scratching its 'innocent' behind against a tree, what would
a 'guilty' behind be like? Well, let's not go into that, especially
when discussing Auden, keep focused on the horse, 'indifferent' to
Icarus falling out of the sky – but it wouldn't be indifferent, this
horse, because it wouldn't have seen – if you've ever looked at the
Brueghel he claims he's writing about you can see the horse not
seeing – and not seeing is not at all the same thing as being
indifferent – and as for Auden in his bar on 39th Street or
whichever New York street he was on, brooding on 'the low,

dishonest decade' – decades can't be low or dishonest, it's a crap historian's or journalist's phrase, OK between blinks but falling apart the moment you bring a spot of attention to it, ask a few questions – how does he rate himself in terms of lowness and dishonesty, as he sits in his bar on 39th Street, that's a question, a real poet's question, also what's he drinking, how much has he drunk, what about his friends – people he knows something about – what are they up to, where are they in fact, with the bombs about to fall, etc., and as for 'Stop all the Clocks', all I can say is it's the appropriate poem for the film, *Weddings and a Funeral* – no, that's not fair, the poem on the page isn't as bad as the poem in the film, the page poem is written as a blues number, it's got a real jump and beat to it, the film poem rolls out like a sermon, reverential and syrupy – and anyway, I've got to face it, almost everybody I like and a lot of people I admire, like and admire Auden, I used to admit as much as I nagged away at Ian, nagged frenetically away, even claiming once I had evidence to prove Auden was autistic – what evidence? Ian asked, – well, I said, he liked to pick his nose and eat it in front of people, and then, well, the poems! I said triumphantly, take 'In Praise of Limestone' and off I went – 'Actually, Auden stinks,' he said, out of nowhere, during one of our very last conversations, 'but his forms, you see, the way he could play about with forms' – and that was it, for him, as a practising poet there was an astonishing skill to be admired and studied. If you weren't a poet and were after meaning, sense and feeling you went to, for instance, Wordsworth on the one hand, Pope on the other, but if you had a technical interest in rhyme schemes, etc., for their own sake, and for the sake of your own practice, then Auden was worth your while – and so we left it at that, for the rest of his life, or at least of my time with him.

TERRITORIAL IMPERATIVES

It is raining – more accurately it's just finishing raining, all the colours washed out, the beach, the trees, the lawn, looking dun-coloured, drab. In spite of the rain the predators were down in the early hours, marking their beds and chairs with towels that are now soaking – but of course the old hands know that this doesn't matter, when the sun comes out the towels (they're green) will dry out in minutes and there will be their beds waiting for them, all prepared – we've had our own spot, at the back of the lawn, separated from the sea by a path and a low wall – not really a wall as the top is separated from the bottom by evenly spaced little pillars, which leave evenly spaced little gaps, through which you can see the sand, the sea, the rafts and boats, people swimming and of course those three prized spots, one of which I saw the old guy fussing over at 6.30 the other morning – I consider ours to be the best spot in the hotel, really, as you not only have this view in front, but also you can keep an eye on all the people on the lawn – and it's become accepted among the lawn community that these are our places, two beds, one low wooden table for Victoria's beach-kit, and a white stool-like table for my cigarettes and ashtray – yesterday a group of three arrived from London mid afternoon, and took the last three beds, which were directly behind us, OK beds but lacking our versatile view – there was something about them that made me immediately uneasy, a woman of about my age, small, and ginger-grey hair, a pretty freckled face with a shrewd and determined look to it – she had an orange hat which she put on and took off regularly, according to some plan to do with how much sun was good for her head and hair, but she seemed to be doing it almost to the minute, as if she'd worked it out mathematically – I pegged her as the ringleader, a woman of steely calculation, designated moves – beside her was a rather slovenly young woman – early forties, probably a daughter, wearing an unbecoming pink hat, cloche-shaped, that pushed her ears down – couldn't really see her face, she wears very large dark glasses, but her body, white, soft and formless, spills all over her bed, and her green bikini bottom has a touch of the nappy about it – there is also a useless-looking man, husband and father, I assume, who comes and goes to report on his success or failure in accomplishing missions appointed by the other two – he came back to say to the daughter that he hadn't been able to find her sunscreen, went off to look for it again in the small zip bag to be found, the mother said, on a shelf in the cupboard, that's where she thought she'd put it, had he thought to look there – he was already on his way. When Victoria and I went for a swim the mother was training her gimlet eyes on a book – I couldn't catch the title, it blends too much into the background design of the cover – but as I say I had my doubts, my suspicions, and cast a look back at them as we stepped on to the sand, and again just before we plunged into the sea – a lovely swim, lovely and long, out to the rafts, towards the next hotel along, an unhappy-looking place, on the skids I bet, with only one bed occupied, listless waiters standing with their trays hanging down by their sides, and then back to our beach, sliding under the moving ropes for the buoys – I'm very bad at this, always misjudging, coming up so the rope scrapes my back or catches my heel, infuriating as I'm mildly allergic to the algae that accumulate on the rope, and so get stripy little rashes on my back and heels. It's inexplicable, as I swim easily under water, love to be there, under water, and it's also infuriating because Victoria glides under them with a few effortless movements of the hips and arms – it's to do with my being over-buoyant (stomach full of bubbles from diet cokes, probably), I should force myself to dive deeper, not just go a few inches under as I immediately, but without realizing it, bob a few inches back up – but going under the ropes, even when there's a stingy rash to show for it, is part of the fun – so out we came from the sea, full of high spirits and the joys of the sea, had a brisk shower under the palm tree and then sauntered across the lawn to our beds, where I noticed immediately my small, white stool-type table had gone, the ashtray lying upside down on the grass, contemptuously discarded. Of course, my cigarettes and lighter, my personal markers, I'd left on the table at the bar, so theoretically, legally, down to the meanest letter of the law, but against every conceivable spirit of it, I had no clear entitlement, beyond the fact that every one of the lawn's occupants knew that the table was lodged in our territory, and belonged to us – specifically to me – I looked towards the group behind, straight at the boss, and then at the small, stool-type table placed where no small, stool-type table had been placed before – there was a tall full glass on it, a straw in it – then looked again at the boss. She had her orange hat on, her eyes, lifted from the book, stared straight at mine, unblinkingly bold, not to say hard, her lips twitched imperceptibly, her eyes went back to her book, fastened there, as with her free hand she lifted her orange hat from her head and put it beside her drink.

So. So I knew. I told Victoria I knew. This morning I rose at half past seven (thinking 'but what's the use?'), peered down from the balcony through the rain, and saw draped over the backs of our beds three green towels. On the white stool of a table was a small bag, presumably waterproof, and on the other table, the small wooden one, some tubes of sun lotion. I trudged through the rain to some beds further down, laid the three green towels on the two beds and the chair, put down some unreadable paperbacks (literally, they've been used so often as markers, on wet days and dry, that now the pages are stuck together, saving them from being found unreadable for the usual reasons), trudged back to the room, dried myself, joined Victoria in bed, where I lay with my arm under her sleeping head – thinking on the one hand of Auden's utterly ghastly 'Lay your sleeping head, my love/Human on my faithless arm' – what is 'human' doing here, what other kind of head would his love have – better not go into that – 'faithless arm' – '*faithless* arm'!, etc. (the worst thing about Auden, I'm coming to realize, is that his lines stick – how come I can quote reams of him, and only fragments of Hardy? And then to misquote Eliot!) and on the other hand how to punish the squatters on our rightful beds, in a hotel where no dog-turds are available owing to an absence of dogs – but there is a cat – a nice cat, marmalady, but a touch withdrawn – and, oh, monkeys – there are monkeys at the top of the garden, by the tennis courts, but wouldn't I arouse suspicion if I were to be seen scraping up monkey turds? especially if they turn up later under the green towels of the squatters.

I'm looking at them now, orange hat, pink hat and useless husband, sitting in a row, in our places, facing the sea, reading their books – almost certainly trashy books, from the rapt expressions on their faces – pink hat has just taken off her pink hat, to release a pack of hair so coarsely and bogusly ginger that it must be natural, nobody could do that to their hair deliberately, not at that sort of age, in this sort of hotel –

Mrs Alzheimer is sitting a bit behind them; she is doing a watercolour. Mr Alzheimer is sitting bolt upright beside her, his face wearing its usual expression. On his feet, a pair of enviable blue canvas shoes, beneath them natty white socks that come up to just above his ankles. He has nothing to read in his hands, which are folded calmly into his lap. I think she is talking as she dabs her brush onto the pad. I think I'll get up and stroll behind them, perhaps I'll hear a snatch –

Of course I couldn't loiter, so I only got one sentence. 'Well, why don't you work at it then?' she said, quite ill-naturedly, but I couldn't tell whether she was talking to Mr Alzheimer or herself. I must find Victoria. Time for a swim.

NEWS FROM HOME

I'm a bit shaken. Distressed would be a better word. This afternoon was mainly more rain until about 4.30, when the rain stopped, the sun almost came out, we were thinking of another swim when the telephone rang. It was the receptionist to ask if I was Simon Gray. I said I was. There was a package, she said, just delivered by FedEx. I went down and collected it, puzzled – disconcerted even – the only person who would FedEx me a package of anything would be my agent, Judy Daish, and she would certainly have phoned to tell me it was on its way, and furthermore have told me what was in it – anyway I'd asked her not to be in touch unless she had some good news, which means, if you think about it from another angle, that I'd been in receipt of a steady flow of bad news –

The package was, in fact, a large, brown envelope, which contained a small white envelope in which there was a letter from Harold. He was writing in response to my letter of a week or so ago – tapped it out on his Olympia portable, he said in his opening sentence, warning me of typos and spelling mistakes to come – it is a page and a half long, and on a separate sheet of paper there is a lovely poem by Alan Ross called 'An old man looks at a cricket match'. The first part of the letter contains a few comments about this and that in my letter and then comes at the centre of the letter, at the heart of it, an account, a terrible account of the state of his health, a concentrated paragraph of pain and bewilderment, typed out on his Olympia portable, with poignant little typos but all his misspellings corrected, the words crossed out xxxx and rewritten –

Now I must tell myself that Harold has not tapped out on his Olympia portable an announcement of his death. He has merely put down, with characteristic clarity, the ordeal that he is undergoing at the moment – the fact that he cannot eat properly, cannot drink (even water) properly, that trying to do either causes him great discomfort, and is sometimes physically impossible. The sentence that most disturbs me – us – Victoria and myself – is that his doctors are completely baffled that this condition should have returned, and more ferociously than before.

I shall stop now. I might go on with this in the morning. I might not – when it comes to it, there isn't much to say – the thing about a close and long friendship – friendship, what an odd word that suddenly looks, as I write it down. Friendship.

SHIP AND HOOD

So that's the word I see when I sit down at the table this morning. Friendship. Looks more normal in the daylight, flowed easily out of the nib, and so I can put down brotherhood, and look at it. Hood, what does it mean, the hood in brotherhood. Well, I suppose the ship in friendship has something to do with making – it has an Anglo-Saxon feel to it, *schiffen* or *schlippen* to do with making, could it be? – I was very bad at Anglo-Saxon, considering it a waste of time because it involved a lot of learning, no chance at all of flannelling through the exam, which, as a consequence I nearly failed (this was at Dalhousie University, Nova Scotia). I wish now – as is always the way with these things – that I'd worked at it, so that I could, for instance, know rather than guess that the word *schiffen* means to make, or is a past participle, made – and so avoid having to check it when I get home – I don't believe I'll be able to get hold of an Oxford Concise here at the hotel – so I'll have to settle for the guess, and turn my attention to the hood in brotherhood, about which I haven't a clue – fatherhood, motherhood, brotherhood – sisterhood – other words with hood as a suffix, I can't come up with a single one, but then I am in Barbados, the morning is balmy, my mind a muddle of passingly agreeable thoughts, and dark ones lodging deeply – hood, hood, come on, come on – riding hood, Little Red Riding Hood, why would a little girl walking through the woods to visit her granny be wearing a riding hood, and what is a riding hood – in as much as I can visualize it, I see it as dark and sinister, as sported by the four horsemen of the Apocalypse, for instance, or the Ku Klux Klan, is there something in the story I'm failing to remember, an explanation of Red Riding Hood's wearing a red riding hood, it can't be that Hood is her surname, Red and Riding her Christian (given, they try to compel us to say, these days, in case we offend a Muslim) names – highly unlikely, Red is a name for Irish-American baseball players, Riding as a middle name? Well, I suppose it's possible, no odder than my own, come to think of it, Holliday, though actually Holliday is my third name, not my middle name, Simon James Holliday Gray is how it goes, so Simon James Holliday Riding Gray? I like it – Simon James Riding Holliday Gray? – but it's a translation, isn't it, now I come to think of it, it has a German or Slavic or Scandinavian feel to it – the woodsman, the granny – Grossmutti? – the wolf, the wolf waffle, no, that was Luftwaffe, wolves come into the Nazis somewhere, I'm sure of it – no good going on with this, again wait until I get home, there'll be a book, quite a few books, no doubt, giving the antecedents of nursery stories, as well as all kinds of analyses, Freudian, etc. – disclosing what the wolf really intends when he says, ' All the better to eat you with, my dear' to L.R.R. Hood, or Ms Hood – abandon these futile speculations and take the full word 'brotherhood' in all the meanings it has for you, leave it at that, which is quite enough.

But of course I've started thinking about Piers, over a decade younger than Nigel and me, and dead – how long is it now? four years, five years, that long? The unfairness of it. Though what is fairness – On the day that he was born –

Born. Whenever I remember it, it's always in a slack sort of way, Nigel then about twelve, myself ten and a bit. We're playing cricket on the pavement outside the house, and my mother – *our* mother – comes out. She is wearing a hat, looking elegant and in a hurry. She stops, though, to announce with a smile that she has just given birth to a baby boy, we're going to call him Piers, isn't that exciting news, now she's off to meet Daddy, we haven't seen each other for a long time – this is how the scene idles through my mind, and though it's self-evidently wrong, it's always seemed right enough in feeling – actually, as I think about it properly, I now see that it's a conflation of two memories, the later one, to do with the announcement of Piers's birth, mixed up with the early one, when I was about four and a half, Nigel six and three quarters therefore – we're playing in the snow outside our grandparents' house in Montreal, 4047 Vendôme Avenue, our aunt Gertrude is in attendance somewhere but I can't see her in memory, all I see clearly is Mummy, dressed in her fur coat, carrying a small suitcase, walking hurriedly past us, her face averted. We ran over to her, she stopped, we asked where she was going, she said she was going to get some milk, she really couldn't stop, she said, smiling a smile that meant something terrible, and off she went. Then we were told by Gertrude to go inside, where Grandma was waiting to tell us that the milk, so to speak, was back in England, with Daddy. Gertrude was a small, thin, wiry woman, with a sharp voice, often irritable or exasperated, doing her best against the grain of her temperament and possibly ambitions, to look after her brother's two children, for whom she had little natural affection, I suspect, but towards whom she had a strong sense of duty. Grandma, apart from being short, was quite the opposite, a roly-poly, playful, laughing – sometimes hysterically laughing – magnificat of a grandmother, who perpetually sucked peppermints (to conceal the sherry on her breath, I now know), who adored me, and whom I adored being adored by. She used to tickle me until I nearly fainted, bundle me about the bed, and hold me into her breasts, enveloping me with her wonderfully pepperminty smell, with its magic additive – Grandpa.

Stopped there this morning. Can't write tonight. Too much of the sun, though of course I sat in the shade as always, but then I must have spent a total of two hours in the sea, the sun beating down on an unprotected and salty head, so I'll just sit for a while, drink a diet coke, smoke a few cigarettes, go to bed. Try not to think too much. Probably can't anyway. The inside of my head feels soft and thoughtless, with a muzzy ache going round its rim. Leave a space for tomorrow. Then Grandpa.

GRANDPA THEN

He was in his late sixties when we came to Canada. He was short, he had sticking-out ears, he was bow-legged, he always had his hair crew-cut, bristly grey it stood in a bundle of stubbles straight up from his head. His Scots accent was still as strong as the day he and his wife – good God, I've just this second realized I don't know Grandma's Christian name, let alone her maiden name – anyway, they left Greenock for Canada at the turn of the century. He was a personal secretary to a steel mogul, working in Toronto, or was it Ottawa? from Monday to Friday, returning to Vendôme Avenue late on Friday night, an event much dreaded by me as I occupied his bedroom, and he would carry me from his bed to a sofa in the sitting room, which I found frightening, or to loving slaps and tickles on Grandma's bed, which I found entirely satisfactory, of course, especially snuggling into the doting comfortableness of her – the dread was of the actual removal, the rough, almost violent picking-up, the stiff, indifferent carrying, as if I were logs, the abrupt dropping down – joltingly, if it was on to the sofa, more complicatedly unpleasant, if on to Grandma's bed, never near her, but at the foot, or on the side, in both cases close to the edge. There was no communication between us that I recall, no warning before he jerked me from sleep, no warning before he dropped me –

The truth is – was – that poor old Grandpa wasn't wanted in the marital, and I was, and it was a shortish journey from the sofa to his marital, and my little legs made it often, and what did he have but his bachelor's bed, kept insultingly warm for him by me. He tried his best, though, during the short weekends and vacations, to be a Grandpa, taking us on Saturday mornings to a palatial soda fountain, for ice-cream sodas and milkshakes, and spending half-hours with us in the garden on Sundays, throwing baseballs and Canadian footballs to us – probably rather stingingly now and then when throwing to – at – me. He was a gruff man, reserved, seething with unreleased energy, his bow-legged gait rapid and forceful, 'full of vim', as Grandma used to say, with one of her long, tipsy giggles – well, of course he was full of it, with nowhere to put it, being Scots, Presbyterian, faithful, honourable, etc. – except once, into me, with a strap. He'd been in some other room – his bedroom, perhaps, lying, staring at the ceiling, no, no, it was evening, that was the point, a Saturday evening, past my bedtime, I was frolicking on the bed with Grandma, the game being that she would order me to bed, i.e. the sofa, I would pretend to go, then dart back, slide under the bed, reappear where least expected, allow her to catch me and tickle me into helplessness, be ordered to bed – we were at it for hours, it must have seemed to Grandpa, tormenting hours for him, blissful for me, and jolly, jolly, jolly for old Grandma, the wife he was never not in love with, every second of his life since he'd clapped eyes on her at a Greenock bus stop. He erupted into the room, wielding a strap. He seized me by the nape of my neck, ran me into our shared bedroom where he swung me about with one hand, flailed at me with the strap with the other, yelping out half-sentences to do with teaching me to go to bed when I'm told – time I learnt – Grandma stood at the door, swaying, pleading, crying out with the blows that it was her fault, we were only playing, stop James, please stop – and Gertrude, shocked and silent, grappling with different duties and devotions – to the nephew to which she was an unwilling guardian, to a father she revered, to a brother she worshipped – of course, I didn't really know what she was grappling with, didn't know then (too busy with yelps, screams and sobs of my own) and I don't know now. She'd had a fiancé, a pilot shot down in the first year of the war, but the only photograph she ever showed us was of herself and our father, children at a lake, both grinning in bathing suits that in her case really looked like a suit, he in one with straps over his shoulders – Gertrude gave us our breakfast, lunch and tea, took us to the doctor and the dentist, walked us in our early days to school, read to us in our early days at bedtime, but of Gertrude I know almost nothing – in fact I don't know even that she was an unwilling guardian, she might have come to care for us deeply as Mummy sometimes claimed, when feeling called upon to defend the decision to take us to Montreal after war had been declared and when the U-boats were freshly on the rampage, and then to bring us back just before the war's end, when the U-boats were still on the rampage, but the question here, whether our parents wanted us back or Gertrude and our grandparents wanted us gone, I no longer have a hope of answering. Mummy in later life propounded one or the other, according to her mood – 'No wonder they wanted to get rid of you, is *this* how you behaved?', sometimes separated by no more than a few sentences from 'We had to risk bringing you back when we did, we were missing out on your childhood, you see,' her eyes filling with tears, her voice shaking with what often turned out to be laughter so that – so that really –

Grandpa taught me to swim in the lakes one summer, when I was five. He'd taught Nigel in the summer the year before. That summer he taught me. Held me firmly under my stomach, encouraged me to kick and to strike out with my arms – this wasn't for graceful or stylish swimming, strictly functional, for survival. The moment when he let me go and I didn't for once flounder and sink, but remained in the water, held up by my own mysterious forces and moving an inch or two was the most ecstatic of my life. So Grandpa gave us our swimming, Gertrude gave us our reading, Grandma gave me all the love I needed – and more. 'All you can eat – and more!' reads the sign outside some of the hamburger joints in the States – but the comparison doesn't hold, to be offered more hamburgers than you can eat induces nausea. More love than you need – well, there's no such thing, in a Grandma's case, my

Grandma's case. My appetite grew by what it fed on, needing more cuddles, rollings about on the bed, swallowings up in round flesh and rich pepperminty and something else smells – and a jealous Grandpa to boot.

We were sent back to England some months before the war ended, but I remember almost nothing about it – of the leave-taking, last cuddles, etc., nothing of the trip to New York, or of being put on the boat by Grandpa and Gert, of the journey itself nothing, until I come to my mother's face, appalled, as she took in the two thugs, crew-cut, ears sticking out, with Canadian accents, who'd come back in place of the English moppets she'd checked up on outside 4047 Vendôme Avenue, on her way to get the milk.

From Grandma, Grandpa and Gert we got Christmas cards and birthday cards, five dollars inserted, until we'd grown up. I visited them once when I was in my early twenties, stopped by for lunch on my way from London to Halifax, Nova Scotia. Grandma was in her mid-seventies, and though there was no question of my getting any rollings about on the bed, or ticklings and hysteria, there was still something in her eyes when she looked me over from top to toe, and then took my hands in hers and gave them a long, suggestive squeeze. 'Oh, I can tell from these you're a writer,' she said, 'these have never done a day's work in their life, and don't intend to.' And she turned her round, shiny old face up towards mine, and laughed into it a great gust of peppermint and what I could now identify as sherry, which made me feel quite dizzy, really, and a little loose at the knees. Apart from that, I don't think she spoke much. Grandpa sat at one end of the table in the kitchen, I sat at the other, his two women sat between, one on either side, though Gert didn't do much sitting, she either served, or stood waiting to serve, a Black Cat or a Craven A held between fingers that trembled. Her face was gaunt, her eyes sunk, her voice hoarse, she seemed very ill, but of course I didn't know her well enough to ask after her health. Grandpa and I did most of the talking, he asking thoughtful, Scots-type questions in his strong Scots accent about the make of the aeroplane I'd flown in from London, the state of the English economy, which I answered with lies and guesses and other Cambridge mannerisms. I didn't think of how he'd once thrashed me with his belt – perhaps he did, though, and wistfully. The three of them died a couple of years later, within months of each other, from unrelated illnesses, although they were probably connected deaths in the sense that whichever had gone first would have been the crucial prop removed, the other two would follow, of necessity. Gert was the first, of cancer, in her early fifties, Grandpa next at eighty-six – working almost until he died, his employers under the impression that their Scots dynamo was still in his sixties; then Grandma of liver, I suppose, a bit more lingeringly and expensively than the other two, although Grandpa's life savings were almost entirely used up on Gertrude's medical bills, which were enormous – he must have believed that property was theft, or a waste of capital, or provided career-debilitating security, anyway, for whatever reason, he rented every house they lived in, including 4047 Vendôme Avenue, and he died penniless. Grandma's bills in a nursing home were paid for by their son, my father, who, having moved back to Canada himself (Halifax, Nova Scotia), was able to afford them. I suddenly find myself remembering other stuff about our time in Montreal, to do with Gert and her Black Cat which was cork-tipped, and about smoking, that I was a heavy smoker in Montreal by the time I was seven, but I don't have the desire this evening – a lovely evening, sun hovering before sinking, a light breeze, the sea a trifle turbulent from an earthquake somewhere or other, I'm going down to the beach.

Just back. The red no-swimming flags are up. I decided to ignore them in favour of a bit of rough and ready surfing, using my stomach as a surfboard, well, surf-tub, getting a kind of bum's rush onto the beach, where I rolled onto my front, heaved myself to my feet, lunged back into the waves. I did it lots and lots of times. Then saw in today's (yesterday's) *Telegraph* a review of Harold's sketches at the National, in one of which he also performed – reviewer said Harold had lost a lot of hair, looked frail, had also lost some of his commanding presence – was this necessary? Could he not simply have reviewed the sketch, with a courteous nod to his acting? but today's today, even in yesterday's *Telegraph*, and we don't do that these days.

SIGNIFICANT SPEECH

The dreadful thing about this most necessary (so I believe) holiday, is that I can't afford it. I'm overdrawn at the bank, in debt all over the place, have pretty well no income. On the other hand I don't really mind. Some years back I would have minded. But some years back I could have afforded it. Even the bar bill, when I was a four-bottles-of-champagne a day man. But that was some years back. Now I don't have a bar bill, worth speaking of. But even though it's not worth speaking of (diet cokes, fruit juices now and then) I can't afford it. But as I don't mind, why think about it? Think instead about the –

Alzheimers, really? What about them? Yes, the thing is that there they were, the two of them, this late afternoon, sitting at the far end of the bar, where it opens out to an expansive view of the sea, the waves crashing a few feet below, against the rocks and the wall. They were facing another couple, elderly, English, with a table not exactly between, because the other couple were sitting at it, the Alzheimers quite a bit away from it, which gave the impression that the Alzheimers, formal and stiff, were being interrogated. Or that they were doing the interrogating. My plan (which I executed) was to drift around them in a roundabout fashion, picking up any audible scraps of chat. I had to get quite close to hear anything, as the sea was loud, the voices low and the conversation, when the non-Alzheimers were speaking, free flowing, unstructured, and when you could hear it nearly meaningless. In fact, the first sentence I understood was spoken by Mrs A. Her voice had a bark to it – her social voice, I suppose – and she has a tendency to 'ink' her 'ings', as for example, now, as she said: 'You weren't thinkink of stayink there, then?' They chattered back that no, they'd had a good look around, it hadn't suited them, but they'd liked the pool, the grounds – obviously all this about a hotel that's recently opened to incredulous applause on the island – applause because it's smart, handsome, comfortable, etc. and so forth. Incredulous because it's plonk in the middle of Barbados, miles from the sea, and who wants to be in Barbados if you can't be up to your waist within minutes of leaving your room – 'I wouldn't stay there,' said Mr A, in a clear judicious voice, 'not if I can be staying here. All this –' he gestured with his stick, stiffly but quite dramatically towards the vast and billowy etc., over the rim of which the sun etc. – 'all this! *And* we've got a pool,' he stabbed upwards with his stick – 'into the bargain.' Mrs A looked at him with controlled lasciviousness. 'That's right, he didn't like it at all, did you, Humphry?' Humphry, whose accent I now identified as Canadian, confirmed that no, not at all, he hadn't liked it, wouldn't stay there for a single night. 'Nice lunch, though,' he added, 'worth going for a lunch.' So. So. Mr Alzheimer hasn't got Alzheimer's. Not only is he capable of speech, he's capable of opinionated speech. Of course, the fact that he's Canadian might have given rise to the misunderstanding, in that one sometimes feels, not that Canadians can't remember, but that they look and behave (some of them only, of course, and even they only sometimes) as if they haven't got that much to remember – not burdened by too much history (Europe), nor animated by too much aspiration (USA) might be a rush-to-judgement historian's way of looking at Canadians, though about the quickest, funniest, wisest man I know is Canadian – though actually he's Jewish, his name is Louis Greenspan and basically he comes from Poland – his father was a rabbi who specialized in circumcision (he developed the knack shortly after arriving in Halifax, Nova Scotia, and discovering that there was a shortage of rabbis in this field) – in 1938 he was only just restrained by members of his family from returning to Poland because he'd had enough of Canadian anti-Semitism – which doesn't mean that he preferred the German variety, only that he hadn't much of a nose for the future. But to get back to Humphry – no, there's nothing to get back to, really, except an entirely fresh burst of speculation – Humphry is a super-rich Canadian recovering from a stroke – how about that? suits the rearranged facts – and his wife, the late Mrs Alzheimer, is probably, given her displays of almost gloating physical affection, only recently his bride – so Humphry is a widower, and she – given also the impression she conveys of long familiarity – possibly an employee – secretary, perhaps? Long-time nurse of the long-time ailing now defunct first Mrs Humphry – or – or – well, there's another guest we should take a look at, turned up this morning in a red cap, white blouse, red pantaloons, red woollen socks, and black sandals – turned up on the beach in this outfit, a man of about fifty, a New Yorker from the sound of him, and quite definitely the sort of chap most easily described by the sort of word

one isn't allowed to use any more – faggoty, queer, pansy, etc. – there
are distinctions between them, I know, but he sort of blends them
all together – oh, hag-fag probably gets it all in a hyphenated one,
as he hangs out with a dwarfish and dour middle-European lady,
who a few days ago was hanging about with a young – well, much
younger than she is – rather jolly woman whom one would have
taken for her niece if they hadn't spoken to each other in English,
with thick but distinctly different accents – hag-fag, by the way, had
a natty little camera with him, which he pressed into the hands of
one of the waiters, then perched himself on the wall, the sea behind
and virtually under him, and posed for a picture of himself. Just
himself. In his red socks, black sandals, red pantaloons, white blouse,
red cap – his hag abandoned under a palm tree on the beach – I'm
going to stop this. I'm coming to the end of the pad, we go home
the day after tomorrow (Monday) so I shall leave the remaining page
open for last-minute pensées – or leave it blank, perhaps.

As Mr A passed me in the bar after lunch he pointed with his stick
to the ice bucket which contained a bottle of water, and said, 'I can
see you're a man who knows how to live,' thus reviving memories
of myself of six years ago, sitting at the same time of day with a
bottle of champagne in the bucket. Mrs A was nowhere in sight. So
Mr A from immobile and mute, to garrulous and roaming. I found
more grace and nobility in him when he had Alzheimer's.

When I was changing into my swimming trunks in the bedroom,
I caught my naked self in the mirror. Great stomach drooping, like
a kangaroo's pouch, though without the opening at the top, thank
God – when I stretched my arms out, their pits seemed to have
dewlaps, or would wattles be the word? Old. Old's the word.

Came across a discarded section of *The Times*, several days out of date – a medical supplement, in this issue dealing with cancer of the oesophagus, Harold's cancer. Horrible reading – hideous statistics. Hope Harold doesn't come across it, or he'll think he's a goner. Why would they publish statistics of that sort – presumably the medical profession knows them, and current and future patients will be demoralized by them – they certainly can't be helpful, can they?

Every night there's a lizard, light grey lizard, about three inches long, on the wall of our terrace, chasing a black moth around the lamp. Every night they go around and around the lamp, in loose, zigzaggy circles.

Beside me on the table as I write this last sentence on the back of the last page of the pad, there is an envelope addressed to Rollocks containing some money and a note thanking him for looking after me. I add that I look forward to seeing him next year. Well –

2

LAST CIGARETTES

Well, here I am, back in London, dizzy and faint from jet lag, or possibly from all the usual remedies, etc. that Victoria has pressed on me to counteract jet lag, or possibly from all the cigarettes I've smoked to make up for the cigarettes I couldn't smoke from the time we passed through security at Barbados airport to the time we got out of Gatwick – a matter of twelve hours, most of them spent conscious, not smoking – most odd that I never mind, in fact scarcely notice, not smoking when I'm officially forbidden from doing so, but the moment I'm a free man I smoke virtually double to make up for the long period of obedience. Ian was probably killed by cigarettes, a fate he accepted stoically enough – a wry shrug, a little grunt of laughter – until it was on him. Even then he accepted the logic of it, as a natural consequence of a self-destructive and therefore unnatural habit, but to the end he couldn't or wouldn't stop. Another friend of mine, another close, good friend died from cigarettes – emphysema, in his case – but he tried to stop as soon as he became ill – he spent the six or seven years in which his lungs shrivelled fighting, and losing, the battle against his addiction, thinking that it would follow the same pattern as his battle against alcohol, in which he'd ultimately triumphed – a heroic tussle, it had been, his tussle against alcohol, entailing many squalid capitulations along the way – he was a great presence for me when I had to stop drinking for ever, never ever patronizingly the forerunner, always treating me as I longed to be treated, as the only man who'd ever had to give up alcohol – so he died dry, sober, full of hatred for the old drinking self that had wasted twenty years of his life, and still waging a pitiful last campaign against his smoking self – giving up on his deathbed. It was a chosen death, as a matter of fact, he was offered either a few months lingering helplessly, rasping out short, stabby breaths, or a double or so ration of morphine and an immediate release. It was a decision he made in clear consciousness, to that extent an enviable death, but it was slightly marred, in my view, by his wife's odd sense of style. As he was slipping from the scene, she pressed into one hand a glass of whisky, and between the fingers of the other, a lighted cigarette, thus turning him in the last moments of his life, when too enfeebled to resist but still conscious enough to be aware, into an advertisement for the two things that had destroyed his life. Though I suppose if he'd been photographed and circulated, he might have served as the ghastliest of warnings – look what I've done to myself, and with both hands – she described the doing of it, the getting of the lighted cigarette between his fingers, the curling of his fingers around the glass – she'd poured the whisky in after she'd got the glass firmly settled, she said – I asked her with what tenderness I could muster why she'd done it, well, she said, well, that's how she remembered him in his heyday, when she first met him (both in their mid-forties, divorced, with children), for her he'd been the most glamorous, flamboyant, chain-smoking, whisky-guzzling – and that's how she'd go on thinking of him, that's how he'd like to have gone out, didn't I think so? 'He wouldn't have been seen dead –' I wanted to say, but couldn't, as actually he had been, pretty well – also she was brimming with grief, exhilarated with it, as people sometimes are when they assist a loved one to cross the line, and she had a theatrical background (her father had been famous in musical comedy) and so what could I say – well, volumes, really, but I didn't, hoping that a brief silence would also be a deep and eloquent one. 'I knew you'd approve,' she said, confirming Wittgenstein's remark, which I usually think is nonsensical, that our understanding of the world depends on the way we interpret the silence around us. And mine wasn't even around her, it went down the telephone line, straight at her. But can we say that she misinterpreted it, and thus failed to understand the world, or at least the world inasmuch as I wanted her to understand it, hence *my* world? Am I saying that she misunderstood my world because she failed to understand my silence? But can a silence be mine, or yours, or his or hers, surely a silence down the telephone is the telephone's silence, open to any interpretation, and she decided to interpret the telephone silence in terms of her world (i.e. her grieving impulse to create a glamorous last image of her dying/dead husband) which leads me to assume that *he* must have been silent when she arranged the cigarette and the drink in his hands, incapable one assumes of vocal consent or protest – El Cid springs to mind here, strapped dead on to his horse to lead the charge that drove the Muslims from Spain, played in the film, both dead and alive, by Charlton Heston, who defined the distinction between these two states by being noisy when alive, mute when dead, but actually more eloquent dead than when alive – and you could say that my friend was eloquent in death, but it wasn't his own eloquence, it was his wife's, who offered it up for an interpretation that I completely understood and that I could meet only with a silence of my own which she completely failed to understand but assumed she'd interpreted correctly – though think of it this way, if she'd asked me to interpret my own silence with a simple question, i.e., 'Why are you being silent,

Simon?' most likely I'd have said, 'Oh, I'm only being silent because – because um – I can't think of anything to say – um – just thinking – imagining him there – dying, dead, a cigarette between his – and a glass of Scotch, was it, why Scotch, by the way? His drink when he drank was vodka or gin, though admittedly when those weren't available anything alcoholic would do, I remember his breakfasting once off the dregs of his last bottle of gin and about a quarter of a pint of port, mixed into a coffee mug –' and so from there we would have escaped from the attempt to understand each other's world through the interpretation of each other's silences, by swapping anecdotes about the beloved dead when in his heyday as a smoker and a drinker. *Requiescat.*

All of the above was written – and is being written – onto a yellow pad by a Cross ballpoint pen (pleasantly heavy) held, in the classic handwriter's grip, between the thumb and forefinger of my right hand – which brings to mind Keats's astonishing line from 'The Fall of Hyperion, A Dream', I think it is – 'When this warm hand my scribe is in the grave'. In my case it is likely to be dead in the grave because, in my left hand, held between the two middle fingers in the classic smoker's grip, is a cigarette. But of course I smoke with my right hand when it's not busy with a pen. So I'm killing myself with both hands, although not simultaneously, I'm glad to say . . .

My mother died of cancer when she was fifty-eight. She began to be ill on the first night of my first play, and died during the last week of its run. In accordance with her instructions – 'If I get ill, my dear, I don't want to know that I'm going to die until it's all over!' – she was led to believe that she was suffering from an entirely predictable recurrence of her war-time tuberculosis, and that with rest and patience she would soon be back on the tennis court – she was a formidable player, even in her fifties, smoking not only between sets but between games, and sometimes – when she was serving – during them. (In Halifax she'd taught the young ladies of Dalhousie University how to play hockey, had raced up and down the pitch wielding a hockey stick, occasionally removing the cigarette from her mouth to blow the whistle which hung around her neck – it was an extraordinary and famous spectacle, from which Nigel and I, both students, used to avert our eyes as we hurried past to the library or lectures) – well, as I was saying, when she was dying she was told all that was needed was what was needed the first time she had tuberculosis, patience and rest – though every so often when she was in the middle of a lively sentence, there was a look in her eyes, vague and appalled – the words would stop and she would lie back, – her arms and legs had become sticks, her face gaunt, her eyes sunk, and her stomach – 'My dear, how ridiculous! I look pregnant!' – but she maintained her belief that she would shortly become well right up to the last days, when she was given enough morphine to keep her either comatose or hallucinatory. In one of her last lucid spells she said, 'I'll tell you one thing, Si, I've learnt my lesson! I'm never going to smoke another cigarette.'

My father never learnt his. He died in the same hospital – Charing Cross – under the supervision of the same doctor. One afternoon I came in to find him agitated, knotting the end of his sheet with his fingers, turning his face one way and the other on his pillow, muttering. When I asked him what was up, was he OK, he wouldn't answer at first, then finally whispered that they'd taken his cigarettes, he didn't know what to do to get them back. I asked the matron where his cigarettes were. 'Well,' she said, 'we think his smoking probably contributed to his illness.' 'But you say he's dying.' Yes, she said, he was dying. 'Then why not let him have his cigarettes?' 'Because they're bad for him.' 'But if he's dying –' 'Because he smoked.' But what did that matter now? 'It matters because he shouldn't smoke.' And so forth, for quite some time, until I took it up with the doctor – an old friend of my father's – who countermanded the matron's orders. I sat beside him and held his free wrist as he smoked the first of his recovered cigarettes. He gave me such a smile, a smile of such gratitude, that I felt I'd at last become a son to him, and a bit of a father too. A day later an aneurysm burst, and he began to drown in his own blood. He was saved into a quicker death by his friend the doctor, who gave him a lethal shot of morphine, just as he had done for my mother. Piers was with me for the death. Nigel, flying in from Montreal, arrived half an hour too late. As the three of us stood around his bed, wondering what to do, what exactly was the procedure, etc., a nurse arrived with a tray of food. 'Now eat it all up,' she said as she put it down beside his bed and flashed him a nursey smile. 'Make sure he does,' she said as she went out. 'He needs it.' They took him away eventually, and we took away the things he'd had beside his bed, his spectacles, a book, his package of cigarettes, and a rather bulky gold lighter, that I suppose was a present from someone or other.

I am in my sixty-sixth year and I have smoked heavily for fifty-nine of those years. I began in Montreal – no, I need a break here. Light up, settle back, watch something on television.

YOUNG AND PUFFING

We were part of a street gang run by a girl called Carole, who at nine was three years older than me, and was almost certainly the most beautiful girl, as her name suggests, in the whole world. She was at the centre of numerous dramas which culminated in her hauntingly tragic death – slain by a traitor (usually Nigel) or shot for being a nurse or an Apache princess who strove to bring peace to all the tribes, and always, in the magical moments of her going, stretched out on the pavement of Vendôme Avenue, her small, perfectly oval face and her eyes – I can't remember her eyes, her face, in fact I can't remember anything about her except that her name was Carole, and that I was deeply in love with her. There were six or seven of us in this gang, and I have a suspicion the rest of them, including the girls if there were any other girls, played the robust and manly parts – the murderers, enemy warriors, defenders – while I played the close companion in her life, the tender mourner at her death, the one who at the very end held her hand as she smoked her last cigarette, which I would take from her fingers when her head lolled sideways, her eyelids closed, and suck on mournfully. In those days in Montreal everybody smoked. Grandpa chain-smoked, Gert smoked Craven A and Black Cat – neither of them filter-tipped as filter tips hadn't been invented, but one of them, perhaps both of them, cork-tipped, a strip of cork lining the outside bottom end (the cork making it the bottom end), so that the cigarette wouldn't get stuck to the heavily lipsticked lower lip – Gert wore heavy lipstick in all circumstances. I'm not sure, now I come to think of it, that Grandma smoked – I can see Grandpa with his cigarette, it used to jut out of the side of his mouth, but not jauntily, more as if it were a necessary implement, like a pencil – and I can see Gert smoking, the smoke all around her face, causing her to cough a great deal – she used to cough her smoker's cough through the smoke – but Grandma – perhaps not everybody smoked, after all – but then she had the peppermints –

*

Everybody in the gang smoked, of course. Not that we were allowed to – although it's hard, given that smoking wasn't then thought to be a health hazard, to see quite why we weren't. It must have been a matter of decorum, a marking off of one of the stages of growing up – short trousers, long trousers, cigarettes –

Anyway, our smoking was exhilaratingly furtive, the deep, dark, swirling pleasures of the smoke being sucked into fresh, pink, welcoming lungs, it took me just three or four cigarettes to acquire the habit and you know there are still moments now when I catch more than a memory of the first suckings-in, the slow leakings-out when the smoke seems to fill the nostril with far more than the experience of itself, and I regret the hundreds and hundreds or thousands of cigarettes that I never experienced, inhaled and exhaled without noticing – of course it's a truism that a cigarette is at its best after a swim, after a fuck, after a meal and with the first cup of coffee in the morning – but their specialness is connected to the event, they are context smokes, not relished as the smokes of childhood were relished, which carried with them most of all the whiff of the smoking experiences to come . . . There were financial difficulties. Our pocket money was a quarter (twenty-five cents) a week, out of which we had to buy a comic book – Captain Marvel, or Captain Marvel Junior, or Batman – candy bars, cigarettes. On the other hand, in Montreal, as opposed to anywhere in England, we could get all those commodities – when we got back to England we couldn't believe that rationing was actually rationing, having heard the word only as a muddling threat from Gert when we failed to eat whatever was on our plate – 'If you were in England you wouldn't have that on your plate, because of rationing, so eat it up!' – the muddle coming, of course, from our not wanting it (fish and greens especially, in my case) on the plate at all, so that rationing, clearly intended to sound a bad thing, couldn't help sounding in its particular application a good thing. When we finally came up against the word in its true meaning – in its 'Is this all we're getting?' meaning, 'and you're jolly lucky to get that, I had to queue hours for it, and it's only because I get on so well with the butcher – you're not in Canada now, you know! You're in Hayling Island.' – our mother always said 'Hayling Island' rather than England, and Canada rather than Montreal, for psychological reasons – to make us feel the cramping-downness of our changed situation.

But we knew where we were, and where we no longer were. Canada was Grandma and Gert and Grandpa (a bully over the fish and greens, which he once tried to cram into my stomach by force) and candy bars and cigarettes and comic books, and the gang on the streets after school, and almost no supervision – Hayling Island was no cigarettes except when we could cadge them from the American soldiers based nearby, who also gave us candy bars and even the occasional comic book – and also, in cold weather, lifts to school. They were exceptionally kind, and asked no favours in return. These days their easy generosity and enjoyment of us would no doubt arouse suspicions, possibly even investigations. When they left, about a year after Nigel and I arrived, we spent days searching their barracks for mementoes and trophies. On the floor in a corner I found a yellowed, bloated copy of *The Adventures of Sherlock Holmes*, the first book – book, actual book – I read, and I read it from cover to cover, again and again – so there is that, the most important of all the favours that came my way from those kindly young Americans. It's only now, of course, as I write about them, that I realize how *young* they were, nineteen, twenty, that sort of age, seen now from my mid-sixties when once I saw them from my ten years or so. I wonder if the one who left Sherlock Holmes is still alive. Well, why shouldn't he be, he'd only be coming up to about seventy-five – almost in my own age group, when I think about it, in fact he could have been sitting at one of the tables in Barbados, or sunning himself on the beach, after a successful life in crime, or a famous author, or indeed it could have been Ken Annakin, who directed lots of long, popular films – *Those Amazing Men on their Flying Machines* was one, I think. Annakin was there in Barbados during our first week, a plumpish man with a pack of grey hair springing up at the front and then, mysteriously, down again at the back – some Hollywood coiffeur's trick, I suppose. He always had a few copies of his recently published autobiography on his table at lunch-time, others he'd placed in the window of the small shop, among the bikinis and beach-wraps, etc. If he's there next year I'll ask him if he was in the American air force, and if he was, was he by any chance based in Hayling Island in 1944, and if he was, did he happen to leave behind a copy of *The Adventures of Sherlock Holmes*, and if he did could I take this opportunity to tell him how much I owed him – also, while the thought is with me, should I take copies of my own books to Barbados next year, if we're lucky enough to get there? I feel there is a 'No' to all the above questions – was it Annakin who directed *The Longest Day*, by the way? I think it was. So. Inconclusive. What? What is inconclusive? I don't know.

AM I, IN FACT, INNOCENT?

It was Nigel who put the question directly to our father. 'We want to know if you're withholding our rations.' He did actually use the word 'withholding'. I like to think I supplied him with it, but I don't think I did, he came to it by himself, indignation and suspicion possibly enlarging his vocabulary. Our mother responded with a crisp slap across his chops, or his buttocks, depending on availability, and asked him, how did he dare! – he didn't, after that. Have I put this down yet – Mummy was a zestful slapper and cuffer, the first blows were a shock as Gert never hit, and Grandpa only on that one occasion, when of course it was Grandma he was hitting, she the sinner, I merely the sin, but for Mummy hitting was an instinctive reaction, that induced in us appropriately instinctive reactions – we learnt to duck, bob, weave and skip, so that if she connected we came to accept it as our failure of reflex, just as if she missed she accepted it as her failure – she never followed up, except when really incensed, although she would frequently find occasion to aim a slap again almost immediately, so that some conversations were physically chaotic affairs, punctuated by laughter and exclamations of pain. I suppose these days a mother like Mummy would be spending a lot of time in the courts and jail even, but we live in exceptionally stupid days, nasty and stupid, in which phrases do the work not only of thinking but of feeling – 'an innocent child', we invariably say, when we all know somewhere in our systems that there isn't, and never has been, such a creature. The other day a Frenchman, who dragged his unruly son out of a restaurant on to the pavement and slapped him sharply on the bottom, was reported to the police by passers-by, spent a few nights in jail 'to teach him a lesson', and has to return to face trial. This happened in Scotland, of course, and in Edinburgh, more of course – but some good may come of this, it might teach the French to stop romanticizing the Scots, they only do it to get at the English, with whom they actually have far more in common – at least in terms of cultural achievement, native wit, intelligence –

But what's my increasing distaste for the Scots – I'm half-Scot myself, or half Scottish or half-Scottie, whichever is the most offensive – got to do with the question – what question? Oh yes, is one closer to innocence when old than when young? Well, take your own case – yes, take my own case, am I closer to innocence now, at sixty-five and a few months, than I was when I was eight and a bit? A fatuous question, and I didn't even ask it – I've just checked and nowhere do I ask it, which is lucky as how could I possibly answer it, not knowing what innocence is even, when it comes down to it – on the other hand I did write that it's a state that has to be achieved – yes, I did, alas – but do I really believe that one day, through hard spiritual work, I might be able to say, 'There! Innocent at last, thank God!' when it's quite obvious, virtually a law of nature, that every day I increase the aggregate of bad things I've done and thought, and even though I do fewer and fewer as I have less and less energy I'm still by definition growing less and less innocent, though it also seems to be a law of nature that I mind less and less – scarcely notice it, in fact, thank God! – for instance, I still feel worse about helping Nigel to kill a rat (already dying, probably poisoned, so it was for its own sake of course) when I was eight than about something vile that I did this morning which if I remember it this evening I'll let pass with a wince, if that – more likely a blink – most likely, though, I won't remember it. But supposing our moral systems aren't like our gastric systems or livers, don't just decay but are subject to sudden bursts of rejuvenation, perhaps ahead of me lies an Indian summer of shame and guilt, before the winter blankness sets in – complete indifference to the world and any suffering I've caused in it – which might in some respects – in my calm smile, my steady gaze – resemble the blankness of innocence – I can hear their voices, 'He was so sweet in those last months, so gentle, simple, childlike –' and also the voice they couldn't hear, the thin cold jeer, acid leaking out of the withered bladder of my spirit, who would have thought the old man had so much piss in him, etc., let us not speak of the wisdom of old men, etc. – have I ever met a wise old man, think, think – well, what about the very, very old man who lived on the edge of a cliff, and looking out one day saw a very, very young man poised to jump. So he went out and saith unto him, 'Why, why are you about to dash yourself down to your death?' And the young man saith, 'Well, the world stinks, all its inhabitants stink, there is no good in it, there is no good in me, why should I go on living, why, why?' So the old man saith unto him, 'Come, come into my little hut, and we will talk a while, grant me this wish, at least, for your soul's sake.' And the young man went with him unto and into his hut, and they talked a while, a very very long while, and then they came out of his hut, and they both threw themselves over the cliff. This story was told by the Reverend Stancliffe, Reverend what? Stancliffe, Henry, Thomas? anyway, Dean of Westminster, he told it to the boys of Westminster school, in Westminster Abbey, some fifty years ago. I can't remember anything else about his sermon, except that it began: '"Everybody for himself!" said the elephant, as he danced among the chickens'. It's the only story I know about the wisdom of old men. Blake's God is an old man with angry cheeks. And Larkin's old men – well, we shall find out, won't we?

But to get back to Mummy, 'innocent' is certainly a word I'd use for her oaths-and-blows style of parenting. It came to her perfectly naturally, and was therefore the naturally perfect way to regain full contact with her two sons – after all when we'd last seen her, heading for the milk, I had been nearly four, Nigel five, when we next saw her I was nearly nine and Nigel ten. Of the five years in which she wasn't a practising mother, she'd spent one and some months in hospital with tuberculosis, and the three and a bit before that driving an ambulance on the RAF station where my father was a medical officer – so she'd seen – they'd both seen – a number of wounded, dying and dead young men, and she'd nearly died herself – so a lot of life lived without us, a substantial gap in our relationship to fill, and her clouts, cuffs, smacks, etc. were an effective way of filling it – after the first assault, which took us by surprise and shocked us to tears, we enjoyed, no, loved – loved, although we'd never have admitted it, but what was it we loved? The intimacy, that was it, the knockabout intimacy of it, within a month we were closer to her than we'd been to poor, undemonstrative Gert during the years of her dogged attentions. Our father, on the other hand, only struck once, and that was in cold blood, ritualistically, with a shoe, in the manner of a schoolmaster with no relish for this aspect of his job – though of course no longer an aspect of a schoolmaster's job, but a jailable offence – and here, I swing to an apparently contradictory position.

MR BROWN AND MR BURN

I'm with the jailers when it comes to the schoolmaster floggers – well, not all of them, I was beaten a few times at Westminster, perfectly reasonably it seemed to me, even while it was going on, and though I didn't enjoy the pain, I more than enjoyed the distinction it conferred on me, moving amongst my peers, my bum smarting but my head held high – not a manly figure, nor a boyish one, something decidedly girlish, possibly – a punished princess, yes, the sexual thrill came not with the beating, but after it, in a delicious sense of how I was being perceived, perceiving myself as a self perceived, honoured, desired – which is not, of course, how I may have been perceived at all, contemptuously or disgustedly may have been how I was perceived – depending on the sexual and emotional make-up of the perceivers, some of whom were no doubt capable of complicated combinations of contempt, lust, disgust etc. for posturing and knowing fourteen-year-olds. The schoolmaster I would like to see jailed – like him still to be in jail as I write this, which means he would have done fifty-four years inside as he first set about me when I was eleven, at a prep school in Putney called Glengyle, where Nigel and I were sent after we'd moved from Hayling Island to Oakley Gardens, in Chelsea – was known to me then, as he is known to me now, as Mr Brown. As known to me then he was a very long man, with a long face, long, broken yellow teeth, and a mop of brown hair. For the first term or so he was perfectly pleasant, even, I might say, a bit of a fan of mine – laughed at my jokes and read bits of my essays out, was sympathetic to my problems with maths, and when Nigel and his generation had moved on to their public schools, made me captain of the football team. But then arrived Mr Burn, about whom I have written a few times, and so here, to save myself from the embarrassment of remembering him all over again, let me find the passage – quote myself to myself –

Mr Burn was round and short and he always smelled of sweet powders, different combinations of powders, I suppose, as the powdery smell, and the intensity of the tickle in my nostrils, varied from day to day. His face was always pale, but dully pale from the powder, and his lips were red, nearly crimson. It was like a toned-down clown's, Mr Burn's face, with the large, pale sweet-smelling cheeks, the full red lips, and the coal-black eyes that flickered over you, if you were me, taking in every desirable aspect of your body, and flickering into you to take in all that part of you that you prayed was concealed from all the eyes in the world, including God's eyes, because it was the shameful part of you, the part that was most shamefully you. He had splayed feet and asthma, and would paddle with a soft, rolling gait between the aisles, wheezing as his eyes flickered from this boy to that until they developed the habit of flickering only at me – of course they took in every other boy in the room too, took in their awareness of him. I was the target though. I knew it from my hot flushes, the prickling of my scalp.

Yes, that pretty well holds, at least in that it revives the memory of slightly thrilled nausea in me, <u>now</u>, at the thought of myself as prey to this exotic predator who stalked the aisles of Glengyle Prep, his dark eye fixed under its hooded lid – but what I'm really concerned with here is not the effect he had on me, but the effect he had on Mr Brown, who turned on Mr Burn's arrival at Glengyle from the affable chap I described above into a flogger (he used a gym shoe, his own, and he had a large foot) – no, no, more than flogger, flogging became an addiction, and I was the bottle he preferred it to come in – every other boy he flogged now and then, me he flogged at least once a day, twelve savage strokes – by the third, one couldn't believe one could get to the fifth – added to this the strain of the posture, and the sense of proffering oneself, and the further sense one had of Mr Burn loitering in a corner of the room, or his face at the window – and the sure knowledge that whatever Mr Brown was doing he was doing, unwittingly possibly, for Mr Burn, who never ever laid a hand on me, of course, except tenderly and insinuatingly –

Something of the nature of this relationship I understood at the time, and I still have within me the same understanding, not an understood understanding, but when I try to bring an experienced – more experienced – intelligence to the matter I'm no further forward, the old muddled conviction is, as I say, still there in all its freshness, and the fact is I still have no idea what went on between them, those too utterly dissimilar (and young! young!) men, one tall, thin, boyish and never really very bright but a lover of sports, and without, I feel sure, any lust for boys in him, the other short, portly, authoritative, musical, contemptuous of sports (but he liked to watch me play, turned out in the coldest weather, to watch me put on a special turn of speed for him) – they might have been designed in their symmetrical opposition, by a novelist or a film director – and when they weren't teaching or fondling in the one case, thrashing in the other, they kept each other company. Mr Brown stooping low to catch all Mr Burn's husky murmurings – Mr Brown, as spellbound by Mr Burn's words as I was, had the same thrilled sense that this alien creature had him in its power, and had like me to succumb to its commands – 'But you must give him a flogging, my dear Mr Brown,' I imagine him saying, rather unimaginatively as of course he would have used his Christian name, but then I never knew Mr Brown's Christian name – 'Flog him for his own good, for your own good, my own good, my will be done, my dear and my darling Mr Brown.'

Mr Brown's formalized brutalities became known to my parents, made known somehow and in such terms that they acted swiftly by taking me away within a week and Mr Burn, who might even have been the source of their information, though of course by circuitous routes, came one evening to the house, at his own invitation, to inform them that he'd seen to it that Mr Brown was leaving Glengyle under a cloud, that he, Mr Burn, would be taking me – a remarkable and precocious boy, who needed the closest attention – under his wing. This was reported to me years later by Mummy, who shuddered at the recollection, interrupting herself with exclamations of 'the most revolting, the most repellent – and make-up! I could see he wore make-up!' – I was confined to my room while this conversation was taking place, but I could hear their voices coming from the sitting room, all three of them so familiar, there seemed to be no pauses, rather as if it were a complex musical piece, each voice coming in on an overlap, my mother's loudest, Mr Burn's low, huskily intense, my father's also low, an interrogative mutter, almost. Nigel came into my room, gravely excited – 'What's going on?' he said. 'What have you done?' I hated him for his normality, that he was always untouched by such defilements – a word I use now that describes accurately what I couldn't put a word to then – that the conversation in the room below was a defilement that I had brought on myself by being me – the conversation went on and on, suddenly became louder as it moved to the landing, then even louder as it moved away from me down the stairs, Mr Burn's voice now quite different in pitch, at a pitch I'd never heard before, high, desperate, wheedling, then the slamming of the front door. Then the parents' tread up the stairs. Then my father came into the room. I don't think Nigel was still there. He looked at me gravely, over his glasses. 'He's gone,' he said, quite pleasantly – he had a very pleasant voice, my father – a transatlantic accent that became Canadian while he was dying, Scots – the accent of his childhood – just before his death. 'He's gone. Mr Burn. I think it's time you went to bed.' This was certainly the most serious moment of my life until then, the most shameful – the grave look over the top of his spectacles, the quiet, pleasant voice, as he sent me to bed – he never sent us to bed, Mummy always did that, often with a kick towards our behinds if we dallied or pretended deafness, being sent to bed was a familiar and comic flurry, safe – my father's doing it was like having a sentence passed that wasn't a punishment, more disturbing, more adult, and sad – he was sad, on my account. As if he were banishing me. And next morning's breakfast was filled by our mother with deliberate silences, dramatic awkwardnesses, and when Nigel asked what the matter was, 'That ghastly little man. Your father had to throw him out of the house. But we're not going to talk about him. Or it.' It. It was left unspecified, even when it, in the general sense of the word, was discussed years later – when she talked of Mr Burn it was as if he'd been an impertinent door-to-door salesman who had nearly duped me into buying something disgusting, probably would have succeeded if Daddy hadn't turned up in the nick of time, shown him the door, and as for Mr Brown he was a brute. Yes. But he hadn't been until Mr Burn turned up.

THOSE WERE THE DAYS

I was nineteen or twenty, and on my way from Halifax, Nova Scotia, to Clermont-Ferrand, in the Auvergne, where I was going to be Lecteur Anglais at the Collège-Technique. I'd written to my old English master and Housemaster, Stephen Lushington, that I was going to be in London for a few days, and he'd written back, inviting me to tea. I remember I went into the Abbey and then through the Cloisters and into Little Dean's Yard – it was early evening, and there were boys of all ages hanging around, scholars in their gowns talking, everything as it always had been on summer evenings, in term time, and there was Stephen Lushington with two boys, senior boys, one of them a scholar, and also a man whom I recognized by the tumult in my stomach, the roll of my heart. Stephen Lushington turned his face towards me, and smiled and gestured me over, but of course I didn't see him, not really, I saw only what my stomach and heart –

Well, let me try and see him now, Stephen Lushington. Mr Lushington. My House Master. My English Master. How bizarre those words look, in those conjunctions, House and Master, English and Master, really quite suggestive, but suggestive of what? Oh yes, *The Story of O*, dead book, utterly dead, whips and chains, blindfolds, gags, hoods and harnesses, the whole kit and caboodle and not an erotic sentence, not one rousing and stirring image – and then there was the film. Poor old Anthony Steel with his crinkly hair, his blue eyes and dimpled, doubling chin playing the, yes, English Master, or possibly Milord, strolling loosely about among the naked ladies in a half-open dressing-gown and silk boots, a hopelessly pretty film from a deadly elegant book, only the French, as the francophonies always say – so what about the *maitre anglais*? Or *maestro inglese*, Englisch Meister, don't know any more versions, except the Scots, Hoose Musturr – what am I doing? Well, whatever I'm doing, I'm not seeing Stephen.

He was very handsome, saturnine, with intense brown eyes, and a sharp, growling voice. His ears stuck out a bit, as most good men's do, in my experience, and he was slightly pigeon-toed, like most athletic and nimble men, again in my experience – I myself am slightly pigeon-toed. He enjoyed tennis, was therefore in charge of school tennis, a neglected and somewhat derided sport at Westminster. He'd once been, or wanted to be, an actor, and was therefore in charge of school plays, which he turned from a lackadaisical ritual into the year's major event. I'd say he was a great House Master, if it's actually possible to be a great House Master, but I suppose the qualities of a House Master are mainly defined by what he doesn't do, by his not making up new rules and not enforcing old and pointless ones, by his suppression of bullying, by his not expressing, or insisting on the expression, of some sinister House spirit – our House lost in every sport almost as a matter of course, but nobody minded except the actual losers, which is as it should be. He was relaxed, tolerant and incapable of not treating any boy, however imbecilic, as his equal, and to put it simply one was proud to be in his House because he was its master. He was certainly, most certainly, a great English teacher, the first to read a poem aloud and into life, and into my life – the poem was 'Dover Beach', and actually I don't think he read, I think he recited, as I remember it – his eyes didn't move back and forth along the lines of the poem, they rested on us, above the book's cover, as if he were Matthew Arnold and the poem was coming straight out of him, and not off the page. He was the only adult, outside of fiction, that I wanted to be like – even, perhaps especially, when he now and then took me aside in Little Dean's Yard and said a few sentences, brief, firm, sympathetic sentences, about my behaviour – Dr Garten (French) had reported me for unruliness and insolence, Dr Prague (Maths) for sloth and incompetence – he passed these observations on, and then moved on, with his quick, pigeon-toed gait, into the House, leaving me trying to look to all the other boys in Little Dean's Yard as if I'd just exchanged a bit of civilized gossip with Housemaster, or received some privileged communication. Twins. I would have liked to have been his twin, his subtly younger twin.

I'm old enough now to be the father of the Mr Lushington that was then – a useless but scary thought, inducing not just double but multiple vision, a gang of Grays and Lushingtons at different stages of life, all mixed about, so that, for example, eighty-year-old Gray and thirteen-year-old Lushington find themselves once again standing before each other in Little Dean's Yard, generations apart and chronologically the wrong way round, but still fixed in their original roles, pupil and master, hero-worshipper and hero, old

Gray with his mottled hands clasped humbly behind his back, his wattles trembling with shame, as adolescent Lushington, kindly, thoughtful, bepimpled, hints delicately at certain indelicacies, no doubt the same old indelicacies, in old Gray's behaviour and habits. So there it is. There is what? I think that what I'm saying is that whatever our current ages and circumstances, my first throb of thought or feeling about him is always from that first perspective – if tomorrow he were to loom up from the gutter as I am stepping out of a limo I'd still fall internally into the same posture of guilt-ridden adoration, although only for a second or so, I hope, before holding out an adult and compassionate hand – not that I can really imagine him in a gutter, broken and old, or even old anywhere – I had a letter from him when he'd just reached eighty, describing his recent scramble around San Francisco to get to a wedding – he'd had to run up and down a hill after a tram or trolley, whichever they are in San Francisco, anyway the sort of thing I could scarcely do in my forties – but then I'd have taken a taxi, in my thirties also, so the situation wouldn't have arisen.

But here's the thing, to get back to that – Stephen Lushington was one of the two born teachers my life has been blessed with, a totally unmixed blessing in his case – the other born teacher was the more than mixed, in fact polluted blessing, with whom he was inexplicably standing when I dropped by that evening on my way to Clermont-Ferrand. He not only recognized me immediately, his face, round, pudgy, ten years older, lit up in a most friendly fashion – 'Oh, I know him, we know each other, I taught him at prep school,' and he gave a quite proud smile. 'One of my favourite boys,' he said. I can't remember how the conversation proceeded, but afterwards, taking tea with Stephen Lushington in his study, talking of Canada and so forth, my mind entirely on Mr Burn, I wondered if I should – well, what? Well, anyway, I didn't, merely saying that it had been a surprise, quite a surprise to see Mr Burn there, in Little Dean's Yard, in the sunlight of an evening (though I don't expect I phrased it like that), a dark and pasty creature from my past there in the sunlight – certainly didn't say that – and so he remained at Westminster, in some teaching capacity or other until a boy or two broke down, their parents investigated and he took his leave, under his cloud. So far this all seems simple and morally straightforward, but – let me try and get this clear – what about the then headmaster, who must have presided over Mr Burn's departure? About him, what? after all, with his noble carriage, and gracious, sideways smile, he really had nothing in common with Mr Burn but the paddling walk, which carried him sedately across Little Dean's Yard to the Abbey for morning service, and tenderly around the boys in their dorms at lights-out – they called him Cute – no, no, not Cute, Coote, Coote of course, as in 'as queer as a coote' to be precise, and when those sprightly workaholics, Gossip, Rumour and Scandal, were threatening his reputation, he saved it (along with his job) by marrying into a distinguished literary widow, while poor old Stephen Lushington, on the other hand, well, poor young Stephen Lushington at that time, remember, had virtually no chance of rising to a headmastership, at least at a school like Westminster – though he was married, with children, he'd previously been divorced. Divorced! So there were the three careers – old Coote's redeemed by a late marriage, young Lushington's blighted by an early divorce, Mr Burn's – well, who knows how many further classrooms and school yards he found his way into, how many other elderly psyches his ghost still paddles in, with its lemony this and powdered that and hooded etc. but here we go again, here we go, from Mr Burn to *The Story of O* no doubt, and then we'll have old Anthony Steele in a jiffy, well, dressing-gown – so better leave it, yes, just leave it that it really was all simple and morally straightforward back then – at least when you look at it from the point of view of back then, when those were the days.

BROWN-NOSING AND WHERE IT GOT ME

Dinner with Harold and Antonia at Chez Moi, Harold remote for the most part – sunk deep in the effects of the treatment, which he'd had the day before, but there was an encouraging flicker of the old Harold towards the end, when I was describing a letter I'd just received from a troublesome fan, she wanted to let me know that the secret of my wealth and fame is in my ability, not to write plays, they're pretty ordinary stuff, these acclaimed plays of mine, no, my main ability is to 'brown-nose', I brown-nosed my way through Oxford-Cambridge, then brown-nosed my way into the theatre, where I brown-nosed my way to my present distinguished status by brown-nosing critics, producers, etc. – there was a lot of laughter from Antonia and Victoria, some at the thought that anyone should think I had wealth and fame, some at the way I was perceived by the fan to have brown-nosed my way towards them, when 'I think we've had quite enough of this word, brown-nosing. I don't like it.' Thus Harold – not as forcefully as when robust, but effectively, with a sort of spectral authority – it was the authority which was cheering – though he'd made it a bit difficult to think of any subject that didn't seem to lead naturally and inevitably back to brown-nosing.

Still, it's an odd letter to get, it seems to me, even from a fan – although it's true that I have little experience of fans – and going strictly by results she's on pretty shaky ground, in fact I sometimes find myself thinking that if only I'd had a gift for what she calls 'brown-nosing', or even basic diplomacy – that if only I hadn't said that to this one, this to that one, or hadn't drunk so very much through my late forties, throughout my fifties, I might have – well, what? at least have got my plays returned more speedily by Trevor Nunn, for instance, possibly bits of them actually read by his predecessor at the National, Richard Eyre, to whom I never actually sent them, on the grounds that every time I met him he seemed to wince, in a noble and kindly sort of way, and I felt it would be wrong to trouble him with parcels of plays through the post or with phone calls from my agent – and as for the smaller subsidized houses, oh, the Donmar, now I come to think of it, in the form of young Sam Mendes, when he was even younger Sam Mendes, his face as yet unmarked by appearing regularly in the press, once sent a message through my agent that he was eager to do something of mine and so – fatally for me – asked if we could meet, to discuss it. I told him over lunch about the play I was working on, which I intended very shortly to confer on him – it involved an abandoned wife kidnapping her husband's mistress and keeping her chained in an outhouse, it should be a very well-appointed outhouse, I explained, where she would give her captive rival a literary and moral education, and – as is so often the way with teachers and taught – they would fall in love with each other and – and so forth – I said I thought the basic situation was pretty sexy, didn't he think? especially if we got a really pretty girl to chain – I suspect I gave the impression we'd do it together, find the girl, purchase the chain, one of us wind it about her waist, the other snap the padlock – with the prospect of paying customers, too – naturally I didn't say anything along those lines, explicitly, but perhaps he heard things in my voice, lubricious and salacious things, and saw stuff in my eyes, overfocused and red-rimmed – anyway, he parted from me no doubt hoping our paths would never cross again, and they haven't, although since his Oscar I've sent him an idea for a film, just a few lines, but written out in neat and sober handwriting, to which he replied courteously, in a loose sort of scrawl, but then why should he be careful with his handwriting, he has no need to be. And why rake over these old ranklings, when there are older ranklings that I still haven't finished raking over like – what? The dawn is upon us. Let me greet it with a sleeping pill.

SHIFTY WINDOWS

So there was my father and the one beating, the awkward ceremony of it, but the reason for it – that's the point I don't remember. Was Nigel involved, were we beaten together? – well, not together, sequentially of course – no, I don't think so, I don't think he ever was, it was me solo, but what could I have done that would have caused our father, of all people, a man whose occasional malevolence was issued in little asides, or in thoughtful resignation, or – worst – in deliberately uncomprehending questions – no, there was more than that, there was the jealousy once or twice – a curious episode to do with wellington boots – we came out of the house one Sunday to go for a spin in the car, it was raining, Mummy said, 'Why aren't you wearing your wellies, you fool! Go and put on your boots!' This to me, not to her husband – I protested, as I hated wearing my wellies, they were tight and heavy, impediments – she insisted, my father also insisted, down I went to the basement, plucked out my wellies, and discovered a gash in the heel of one of them – unwearable, as I reported to my parents, showing them the boot. 'How on earth did that happen?' my mother enquired, not conspicuously perplexed. 'I don't know,' I said, not particularly curious. 'He did it himself,' said the father, not at all himself. Steely with anger. 'Did you?' – from the mother. 'No, I didn't,' I said. And I hadn't. 'No, he wouldn't have,' said the mother. 'He wouldn't be so bloody silly.' 'He did it himself,' the father repeated. 'He's lying. Look at his shifty little eyes. His shifty little eyes.' Now this was said not of the moment – he didn't mean that my eyes at that precise moment, in circumstances to do with my boots, were shifting about, but as a general moral fact about me, my eyes were always shifty, I'd been born with shifty eyes as an indicator of my true nature – eyes-as-windows-of-the-soul-shifty. Mummy, my Mummy, was shocked. 'James!' she cried, cried Mummy mine. 'James, how could you!' He muttered something apologetic – his own eyes suddenly shifty and full of feeling – what feeling? Loathing would be to take it too far, I think, looking judiciously back, but whatever it was it gave me, in all my upset, a little jolt of triumph.

A SIGHTING IN PIMLICO

And so we come, in the most natural way possible, to the matter of my father and his Mrs Rolls. She was a small, blonde, lively widow, who worked as his secretary in his Harley Street consultancy – 'Little Mrs Rolls,' my mother invariably referred to her as, or, in poignant innocence – 'Your Little Mrs Rolls, James, phoned, to say that she's made three appointments for you on Wednesday afternoon' – one of them, possibly two, even all three, being with Little Mrs Rolls herself, it was subsequently discovered. I saw them once, when I was walking back from Westminster – I was about fifteen, I should think, and it was somewhere in Pimlico, mid-afternoon, I was about to cross a street and they went past me in a car, Little Mrs Rolls driving, the father sitting staring straight ahead, a perfectly proper little cameo, really – I'd met Little Mrs

Rolls quite often, as for instance when she came to the parents' Christmas party, so I recognized her at the wheel, and him I'd have recognized anywhere, that handsome head (he was said to look like James Mason. James Mason with a pipe – and spectacles), that look of humble, middle-class distinction – but what was there to see? only a small blonde secretary driving her boss to one of his appointments. They weren't laughing, talking, looking at each other, they might almost have been in separate vehicles from the evident lack of connection between them – well, perhaps that was the trouble, that's what I unconsciously grasped, the unlikely stiffness and formality with which they sat – especially him, he gave off the impression of being somehow both lordly and a captive. Or did he? That may be how I see him now, in memory – but what I did notice at the time is that they sat, both of them, as if they were hoping not be observed by someone that they themselves had observed, to wit, myself – well, whether they were or they weren't because they had or they hadn't, the thing is, without actually knowing anything at all, really, about adultery, unfaithfulness, all that, I knew that I'd seen something wrong, that I'd caught him out, and I didn't like it. I didn't mention it, not innocently to Mummy, 'Oh, I saw Daddy this afternoon, it was in Pimlico, he looked quite funny actually, Mummy, sitting there beside Little Mrs Rolls etc.' – or to Nigel – perhaps with him I felt it would be sneaking, even though I didn't understand yet what it was I'd be sneaking about – and I quite consciously resisted the temptation to bring it up two years later, when we'd all moved to Halifax, Nova Scotia –

One afternoon, after lunch, when I should have been trekking back to Dalhousie for a class, she said, 'Si, come and have a drive with me,' and her face had a look, a look that made me at once assume a grown-up posture, manner – we went to the car and sat in it, she didn't start the car, we just sat in the car in front of the house and she told me about Little Mrs Rolls and my father – 'your father' was her term for him on this occasion, instead of the usual Daddy – she cried a bit, and said she'd thought of leaving him – it had been going on for eight years, right up to the day he'd left for Canada – he'd come out ahead of us, to find a house, start his job ('take up his appointment' was the phrase Mummy liked to use) – for eight years James Davidson had been humping Little Mrs Rolls, and she'd never for a moment suspected – not until she'd read her letter – hadn't even suspected when she'd seen the letter, recognized the handwriting, not suspected even as she was opening the letter, why, she'd only opened it because she'd thought it might contain some urgent information that Daddy who was away in Montreal, clearing-up after Grandma's death would want her to pass on when he phoned in the evening. In which case why not wait until he phoned in the evening tell him about the letter, then ask him if he wanted her to open it, or so I would have said, if she were telling me this now – although when it comes to it, it wouldn't have made any difference, if she'd said, 'James, here is a letter from your Little Mrs Rolls, do you want me to open it and read it out to you in case it contains urgent information you need,' he couldn't have said, 'No, you're on no account to open that letter which can't possibly contain urgent information that I need, above all that you need –'

– she'd been thinking of leaving him, she said, yes, Mummy had been thinking of leaving Daddy, what was my view, Si – we were both smoking her cigarettes – I had all kinds of views, most of all an exalted view of myself as an adult, a confidant, the only person Mummy was going to tell, she told me – and I believed her then as I believe her now because in Halifax, Nova Scotia, she had no close friends, was the 'grande dame', a London society queen in exile to a cold colony, she would have been far too proud to confess her situation, that she was a wronged woman, wronged by her husband's secretary, Little Mrs Rolls – too shameful, too thoroughly humiliating! – so I stood in as an adult friend as best I could, allowing myself to feel, for a moving moment, that my father's fate lay in his son's hands, that with a few words – 'Better let him go, Mummy, there's no coming back from that sort of thing' – and so out of the house he would trudge, gone to – gone to where, in Halifax, Nova Scotia? And could Mummy stay, could I stay? Would we have to go back to London, but I couldn't go back to London, in London I'd have to do my national service, which I certainly wouldn't be doing in London, in fact the prospect of Daddy leaving me – her, Mummy, I mean – the family, that is – and there was Piers – how would he manage, fatherless, and so young, there'd just be Mummy in the house, just Mummy and her three boys, only two of them over eighteen! how could she cope, how would we cope, the prospect filled me with panic, 'But why should I?' she thank God! cried. 'Why should I just give up everything! Everything because of her! Let her ruin my life, destroy my family – give her that satisfaction!' He, I noticed even then, didn't come into it much, he appeared to have been merely a vehicle for transporting trouble from Little Mrs R to big Mrs G – my mother was five feet eight inches, by the way, (an ex gym-mistress who'd long-jumped, high-jumped and broad-jumped for Britain in the Commonwealth and Olympic Games, picked up a medal in one or the other, long legs, long, long legs; broad shoulders, long torso, long chin and nose, blue eyes – a big, handsome, dangerous-looking Olympiad of a woman) – in other words, J.D. was a pretty well absent party to his own infidelities, at least in my mother's account – so it ended, this conversation, with my mother suddenly bursting into tears, as she drove me to the Dalhousie Campus – only a few hundred yards from the house – and then driving off, in her usual harum-scarum way, cigarette dangling, to teach the girls hockey, and I went to my classes with, no doubt, the air of a man who was burdened by secrets and responsibilities for an hour or two, no longer than that, because I had my dash to cut, that of the campus aesthete and intellectual with the effete haircut and effete accent and heterosexual eye – and it was really the end of the matter, at least according to Mummy, who reported crisply that J.D. had replied to Little Mrs Rolls's letter with a letter that required – no, demanded – no reply, there was nothing more to be said, the matter never to be mentioned again, wrong of her to have burdened me, my father was a good man who loved – and almost immediately after that there was laughter again from their bedroom that I sometimes caught when I was up early. I was, well, relieved the father was in his proper place, about his proper business, but I had, there's no getting away from it, a most peculiar mixture of new feelings for him – a respect for his 'otherness' – that to himself he was obviously far more than father, husband, pathologist – he had a secret life, just like me, he had desires and needs, just like me, but unlike me he knew how to satisfy them, he was a grown-up, in other words, who knew how to deceive (eight years!), a betrayer. At the same time I felt a moral superiority because I knew something about him that he didn't know (and was never to know) that I knew – I used to imagine it sometimes – telling him that Mummy and I had talked him over rather as if he'd been a difficult child in our custody – and what about that time in the car in Pimlico? – he'd seen me, I knew he had, no, no, don't lie, Daddy, just look at his shifty little eyes, Mummy – careful!, you said to Mrs Rolls, keep staring straight ahead, poppet, did he call her? there's somebody I might know across the street – could just be one of my sons, the middle one, Simon, can't be sure from where I'm sitting – which was in the passenger seat, it's worth repeating.

THOUGHTS ON DRIVING

He loved driving, he was a manly driver, all pipe and speed, puffing out smoke as he took a corner with an emphatic change of gears, jaw tightening with manly irritation when Mummy cried out, 'James, James, too fast, slow down!', another shift of gears, foot lightening on the accelerator, a mutter to the effect that it was all right, he knew what he was doing, – sometimes she'd tell the story about his driving in India, how she was entertaining his superior officer to tea one afternoon out on the porch, a great honour that he'd dropped in, she was naturally very nervous but they were getting along really quite well, he was being most charming about baby Nigel, who was cradled nearby in the arms of the ayah and so forth, really it was all going delightfully when suddenly there had been a roaring and a screeching and a terrible tooting and a car had shot into the drive and down it straight towards the porch and at the very last second had done a jubilant swerve, brake and skid, sending up clouds of dust and pebbles, causing the superior officer to spring to his feet, 'Who is that bloody fool!' he'd shouted, and the bloody fool that bounded out of the car was your father, wasn't he, James? James chuckled through his pipe, did some stuff with the gears, and admitted that it was, yes.

So he really wasn't one for the passenger seat, even when Mummy was driving – she'd been under his command at the air force base as an ambulance driver, so he knew, in spite of her feckless manner at the wheel and her tendency to lively conversation punctuated by vivid gestures with her cigarette, that he could trust her instincts, her athlete's reflexes – still he made it clear from the way he sat, his hands pressed on his knees and his head slightly back, that he found something unnatural in the arrangement, and would for example say, when I answered one of her questions – they were mostly, it's true, rhetorical – he would say, 'You mustn't speak when your mother's driving. She needs to concentrate.'

'But she asked me, didn't you, Mummy, you asked me –'

'No, your father's quite right, I'm not really talking, just thinking aloud, aren't I, James?'

Who would shortly insist on taking the wheel, allowing her, on our long drives down to Cornwall or Devon in the summer, spells of not much more than half an hour or so. I think that though she loved driving, she loved even more the feeling of wifishness when she sat beside him, his passenger. For her, too, it was the natural order of things.

For me, it's second nature to sit in the front passenger seat, being driven by a woman. I like it, for short periods, at least. I like their hands on the wheel, I like watching their foot moving between accelerator and brake, I like the tops of their knees, the stretched out calf, the tension in the ankle – that is, when they're wearing a skirt or a dress. It is less interesting when they're wearing trousers, which they usually do, these days, and when it comes to it, about twenty minutes of being driven is all I can take, my back begins to hurt, and I become nervous of the traffic, and in London of the pedestrians, who I suspect find the sight of a large smoking man driven around by a woman much younger than himself somewhat obnoxious.

Of course my life would have been completely different if I'd learnt to drive. For one thing I'd have been able to drive away from difficult or hateful situations – it's hard, when things have reached rock bottom at three in the morning to walk out, especially if you're in the country or abroad, there is no public transport, no hotel for many miles, nowhere at all to go really except to a field or some woods, lake, river or sea – you'd get lost, possibly drown, be attacked by bats, or die of hypothermia or from terror of the darkness in an unknown place – then the winds, and with the winds would come rain, hail, sleet – and you, crouched in a ditch, unable to get home and say sorry, I love you, make up – so you pretty well have to do what I've done on the occasions that I've walked out – hang about up the road, smoke a few cigarettes, then walk straight back in, only of course you don't make up with an apology and a declaration of love, you pick up where you left off, your dignity insisting that you're only there again because you've thought of something else to say much better left unsaid. But if you can drive off you can drive off until tomorrow, or the next day, or for ever – or so it seems to a non-driver. The freedom I've missed, in other words – but how can I calculate that against the freedom I'd have lost in jail, for drunken driving, dangerous driving, homicidal driving. Character is destiny. Mine is the character of a non-driver. And remember the other party knows it too – especially if the other party is a woman, and a driver, which she always is, in my case.

J. Daddy, MD, although a driver, couldn't drive himself away from his Little Mrs Rolls, and out of her life. She ran his office, she sometimes visited his house, she knew his secrets, indeed she was one of them – she had his telephone numbers – indeed she was one of those, too. To drive out of her life he'd have to have driven out of Mummy's life and the lives of his three sons, Nigel, Simon and Piers, then set up as a general practitioner in a faraway country, under an assumed name, a forged passport – well, how did he break it to her then, tell her that after eight years he was off, and thank you?

Well, he could simply have said that he'd decided to end the affair, no hard feelings please, he'd give her the best possible references, find her another pathologist, let's get on with our lives. Which would have required courage.

Or he could have explained that his finances were such (and they were) and his tax burden such (and it was) that he had no alternative, it broke his heart, but to apply for a job in Canada (which he did), where taxes were low, and incomes for pathologists high. Only fair to his family, he could have said. Furthermore he could have pointed out that he was legally still a Canadian. He'd be going home at last. His parents were now very elderly. He should be near them in their twilight. Yes, he could certainly have said that.

And then he might have said that when he'd settled down, sorted it all out, she could come over too! Why not? She could be his secretary again, everything exactly as it had been, except that it would be in Halifax, Nova Scotia, and not in London, England, that would be the only difference when it came down to it. Yes, don't cry, don't cry, join me when I've settled down, we'll write of course. Yes, I bet that's what he said.

WHAT IS THAT MESS?

During the period of my own adultery I frequently hovered on the verge of suicide – no, not suicide, something more violent, more of a sort of self-homicide – what I wanted really was to seize myself by the back of the neck and dash and dash my head, until my brains were out and I was over and done with. On the other hand I didn't want to be dead. One of my plays was previewing in Guildford, a light-footed (I hoped) though melancholy piece about, well, adultery as a matter of fact. I would taxi the forty-odd miles to rehearsals, sitting carefully in the middle of the seat so that I kept an equal distance between the doors, feet pressed against the floor to give myself either leverage or stability, torn between the desire to fling myself out on to the motorway and be mangled under the traffic – the nursery poem throbbing through my head, oh dear mama, what is that mess, that looks like strawberry jam, hush, hush, my dear, 'tis papa, run over by a tram – so an overpowering desire to turn myself into strawberry jam on the one hand, and on the other an obdurate determination to continue existence as I knew it in the here and now of the taxi, i.e., more gulps from the bottle of Glenfiddich in my lap, more puffs on my cigarette, so just one more gulp, one more puff, then a lunge sideways for the door handle, a swift jerk and out with you – but first a last gulp, a last puff, then one more of each and then reach for the door handle, puff gulp jam jam yesterday, jam tomorrow but never jam today gulp puff jam etc. until there was the theatre, all those actors to boss around, and nothing to worry about until it was time to call a taxi for the trip back. Nowadays of course the situation couldn't arise because you a) can't drink in a taxi, b) can't smoke in a taxi, c) can't open the door while the taxi is moving.

THE OTHER WOMEN

Mummy was a middle-aged woman of the middle classes in the middle of the twentieth century, who would certainly, and with complete truthfulness, have described her marriage as a happy one, a very happy one – perhaps the news of Little Mrs R acted as a challenge, put her on her mettle, perhaps her inherited instinct, or her received wisdom, was to believe that it was always the woman's fault, the women's fault, not just Little Mrs R's, but hers, too – after all, if she couldn't keep her man! – so she kept her man, and I'm pretty sure the subsequent pleasures weren't only his, in fact the laughter from the bedroom was mostly hers, even if I sometimes imagined a male purr running under it – well, why not purr, how could he help purring, old J.D., when he had an even more loving wife to show for his eight years of adultery – really, quite worth the effort – a happier man in a happier marriage.

But it wasn't, as it turned out, only Little Mrs Rolls, his secretary, there was also BoBo Carew, his wife's best friend, his best friend's wife – Nigel gave me this news not many years ago, decades after the death of all parties – and of some of their children too – I suppose he'd held it back from me for much the same reasons as I'd held back from him what I'd seen in the car in Pimlico, but now here it was for my consideration, that he'd surprised them when he came home from school early one afternoon, met them on the landing coming out of the bedroom – out of Mummy's bedroom is how I see it – both of them flushed, holding just-lit cigarettes, and Daddy, devious old devil, said, 'Just showing Mrs Carew something in the bedroom.' Yes. 'Mrs Carew.' That's how one's parents referred to their closest friends, when in their company in front of the children – to each other, in front of the children, it was BoBo this, BoBo that, but to the children: 'Just showing Mrs Carew something in the bedroom.' Mrs Carew was almost onomatopoeically a BoBo, a large, round, soft, hoarsey, chuckling sort of woman, as tall as Mummy, but with enormous breasts – boobs, actually – who, as poor old Mummy, flat-chested, used to say proudly, 'worships your father', not knowing to her dying day where and how or with what –

So, to my certain knowledge, J. Daddy was bonking three women, Little Mrs Rolls, BoBo/Mrs Carew, and mother. Or is it more accurate to say he was being bonked by two and bonking one? No, bonking two, because there was also Mummy's cousin, Betty, also always referred to as little Betty, but in lower case, somehow – I'll try to work this out – yes, the Little in Little Mrs Rolls was almost a title, anyway a social distinction, Lady Rolls, as it were, but at the other end of the social ladder, which would go, as we ascend, Rolls (chambermaid, etc.), Little Mrs Rolls (widowed secretary etc.), Mrs Rolls (married, middle-class, unemployed etc.), Lady Rolls (wife of an industrialist, etc.). – Mother, by the way, would have liked to have been addressed, and referred to, as Mrs Dr Gray. But if the 'little' in little Betty wasn't a social categorization, exactly, as the Little in Little Mrs Rolls was, it nevertheless declined her as an inferior family member – she was a widow, impoverished, with a son to bring up, on top of which she was in fact physically little, seeming to be roughly half my mother's size when they entered a room together, but in other respects very like my mother – especially in her legs, long (in proportion) and shapely, which she enjoyed exhibiting, stretching them out and flexing the calf muscles as she sat chattering out family history, interspersed with compliments to my mother about my father, compliments to my father about himself, compliments to Nigel and myself for having our father for a father, all the while stretching and flexing her legs, which the main subject of her compliments, pulling on his pipe in his armchair in his corner of the room, glanced at now and then, with a pathologist's, or perhaps a pathological, eye.

Little Betty knew all the family gossip, all its history – in fact knew almost every family's gossip and history, able in the course of a single sentence to make a sequence of connections that reminded one of those 'begat' stretches in the Old Testament, verse after verse of who begat whom who begat whom, etc. – so little Betty, 'Oh yes, well she married a Flyn, Jack Flyn, who was the nephew of one of the Tomkins, Lionel, the one who married Elsa, who was the daughter of the son of Lord Dundoodle of the Lancashire Dundoodles, Henry Dundoodle' – on and on she could go, even to me in my teens, I would be listless and irritable after the fourth or fifth name, so that when she came to talk about my own family (hers too), I only listened here and there, almost accidentally – except of course when she told how Mummy and Daddy came to be married – 'Your aunt Deirdre, you've never met her have you, no, of course you wouldn't how could you, well, you see' – and there would follow an enormous confusion of coughs, names, irrelevant antecedents, descriptions of Daddy in the prime of his young manhood ('though being older suits him even more') with pauses for an exhibition of ankle and calf, out of which it was possible, after several hearings, to trace the lineaments of the story:

A LITTLE FAMILY BACKGROUND

Daddy came from Canada to England on spec when he was twenty-five years old, a qualified MD who hadn't yet practised. He answered an ad for a locum in Holloway, North London, at the practice of my maternal grandfather, George Holliday, who was also, of course, little Betty's uncle. The younger daughter, Deirdre, was on the premises, a quick and lively young woman of twenty or so who, little Betty said, was very pretty, though nothing like as attractive as Mummy, and not nearly as athletic. Inevitably and in no time, in a 'mere jiffy' as Betty put it, Daddy and Deirdre were engaged, or 'the next best thing' – little Betty didn't say exactly what the next best thing was, though one has a good idea of what it might have been for Daddy, given subsequent evidence. No doubt – well, let's assume, anyway – that the next best thing would have given way in due course to the best thing, if it hadn't been for Mummy, then a games teacher at a school in Shropshire, who came home for her holiday – what little Betty delivered at this stage of her account was a terrible clutter of hints and innuendoes mainly to do with the instability of Deirdre's behaviour, the trouble she caused – 'she was a bad loser, you see, your aunt' and of course her drinking, 'she got that from your grandfather'. Mummy and Daddy got married in another mere jiffy, and headed straight off to India, where Daddy joined the British army as a medical officer – actually, he probably joined before they left, it would have been more sensible, I think. Deirdre followed them out, but was sent straight back for generally hopeless behaviour – 'flirting and drinking and making a name for herself all over the Punjab' – or wherever. What I know of the rest of Deirdre's story amounts only to this: she married a solicitor from Nottingham, had two children, became a lying-about-in-the-gutter sort of alcoholic, was divorced, prohibited from seeing her children, went into lodgings or perhaps a hostel in Nottingham, was frequently stored for the night in a cell at the local police station, and died of cirrhosis, in her early forties. Nigel and I never met her, but we heard her voice some Christmases if we answered the phone – she was invariably drunk and crying, incomprehensible – Mummy would send us out of the room and she would be, some years, hours on the phone, reappear looking fraught and slightly saintly. 'Poor Deirdre, she really is too, too' – Father would grunt, suck feelingly on his pipe – 'Your aunt gets a little carried away at Christmas, a little the worse for wear.'

So there it is. However little Betty muddled and slanted them and blurred them with coughing fits the facts are clear, my Mummy stole my Daddy from my Auntie and lived happily with him until she died – whereupon little Betty became the second Mrs Dr Gray, a position she'd always coveted, as she admitted on the day of her wedding, 'I was in love with your father from the first moment I saw him in the surgery in Holloway – but as long as your mother was alive – I mean! Good heavens I couldn't compete with your mother, there could only be one winner, with your mother!' as she stood on the tips of the toes of her lovely pins, offering her cheek for cousinly kisses from her three tall stepsons. 'You've got to get me away from that woman,' my father whispered a couple of years later as he lay in bed in their flat in Menton – 'She was always a mistake.' His big toe was gangrenous and stuck out from under the sheets. It looked so dead and so painful that I wanted to cry. 'Yes,' he said, 'she did that.' I knew that he was speaking metaphorically, but I asked him anyway, how she'd done it, how had she poisoned his big toe? She never stops, he said, she never stops. Yakity-yak, yakity-yak. He gestured contemptuously towards the living room where she was on the telephone, talking to the doctor. 'Mon mari, vous savez, je vous dis encore et encore, comprenez-moi, mon mari, il est malade, il est poisonné sur le pied, le pied de mon mari est très malade et poisonné. Vous devez toot sweet visiter mon mari' sort of stuff – on and on she went, on and on, while he smiled at me in ghastly triumph, as if we'd caught her spooning strychnine into his food – but when she came in and said the doctor couldn't come until evening, she'd done her best, she'd tried everything, but it was no good, he wouldn't come, not until the evening, and then began to fiddle despairingly about the bed, tucking him in and so forth, he took her hand and patted it, telling her to calm down, he was going to be all right, after all he was a doctor, wasn't he? – which made her swell up with a mixture of pride and hope, and say yes, of course he was, and more than just a doctor, you know, she said to me, he's a pathologist too, aren't you, James? She sat on the edge of the bed, talking, coughing and exclaiming as she clutched his hand, and he lay there grunting, nodding, dying – well, there was a long history between them, all right. One thing leads to another. That's my point. Perhaps it was his too.

What point? Perhaps our implicit point, Daddy's and mine, is that he was always there for the taking, by the woman of the moment – first Deirdre, then good old Mummy – and good old BoBo, and little Betty here and there, now and then until she became full-time – although here's a thought, where was she, on the afternoon of his death, we were there, his three sons, she was there most of the time on other days, she'd been adhesively at his side when I moved him from Menton to a nursing home in Nice, then from Nice to the Charing Cross Hospital, in fact she caused confusions at every point, especially in Nice, where she drove doctors and nurses to distraction with her disorderly monologues – 'like a flight of starlings, little Betty's conversation,' Daddy used to say to the first Mrs Dr G. – but she loved him, with such utter passion and devotion – and that gold lighter must have come from her, now I think about it, brought to him in Charing Cross, probably just after they took away his cigarettes – yes, well, there you are, that was her sense of timing, at least with him – no doubt she'd gone off to perform some elaborate but useless chore on his behalf, and so missed the moment – or perhaps missed it on purpose, because she couldn't bear to be there at the moment when she became a widow for the second time. Actually it would have been for the third time if the man she was engaged to after her first husband's death had lived to marry her, but he was killed – or so the story went, as told by Mummy – about half an hour after he'd proposed. He'd popped the question while they were motoring through Surrey – why do I write Surrey? I hadn't remembered Surrey until I began to write it down – well, assume Surrey, at least one of the home counties, a busy little town on a busy day, say midday, driving down the high street – well, wherever, whenever, he'd popped the question she'd been waiting for, she gave him the answer he wanted, and then she'd told him to stop the car at a telephone kiosk, she simply had to tell her news to – I don't know, not Mummy, because Mummy would have told it from her point of view, wouldn't she? and described the conversation – whomever. He stopped the car, she got out, crossed the street, entered the kiosk, put in her two pennies, dialled – 'Hello,' she'd said, 'Hello, it's Betty, I've got something to tell you! My dear, he –' etc., etc., and etc., and etc. – and in the car her freshly minted fiancé, driven at last past endurance, or lust, or longing or – just leave it at impatience – as he saw more pennies dropped in the slot, and then more pennies – perhaps a sixpence, or even a shilling, you got an awful lot of talking-time for a shilling, back then when shillings existed – leapt out of the car – and here's the thing, the little Betty part of it, she was so deep in the news of her impending marriage that she didn't take in that not far away the other party to it had been crushed to death under the wheels of a lorry, didn't take in the arrival of the ambulance, the police, the departure of the ambulance, the police – so when at last she headed back to the car, and found it empty, she simply got in and waited – 'Poor little Betty,' as my mother used to say. 'She's had rather a sad life, when you think about it. Of course I know she bores you to death, James, but even so, you're fond of her really, aren't you?'

God knows what he left behind when he came from Canada to England at the age of twenty-five – the same sort of pot-pourri as he left behind when he went back to Canada –

Bound and gagged in Montreal. I'm leaving this as an aide-memoire for tomorrow, when I start again.

A SUNDAY NIGHT AT ORSINO'S

Had dinner with the Waldegraves, William and Caroline, at Orsino's, as we usually do on Sundays. At the far end of the restaurant were Harold and Antonia (as they usually are on Sundays) with a couple of friends, I couldn't make out who. Our conversation was mainly about how a husband should deal with a man who has insulted his wife – some drunk had recently abused Caroline at a dinner party – William, who is an ex Tory minister with progressive views but of ancient lineage, said that in the good old days he would have challenged him, no alternative – or had him horsewhipped, I suggested, because I always like to say the word – horsewhip – generally thinking of a certain theatre critic, who in certain lights does look a bit like a horse, spavined and with dripping, twitching nostrils from his cocaine habit – a horse on horse, in fact – and although for obvious reasons I wouldn't fancy the job of horsewhipping him myself, I wouldn't mind having it done for me – it was a lively conversation, but my attention wasn't fully on it, it was on Harold who several times had to leave the restaurant, walking with a willed step, in an uncertain but straight line, keeping a distance from our table, as if to avoid anxious questions, the first time up the stairs to the lavatory, the next three times out on to the street – and he did look so bravely determined, each time, each time pale, frail, most of his hair gone, his feeble but obstinate tread carrying him out, then back in again, to his far table the length of this long restaurant, it made the heart pucker – so when I got back I wrote him a card, saying that I'd seen he was in distress, hadn't known whether he'd wanted a touch of support or had been trying to escape, what about lunch – I have in fact entirely given up having lunch with friends, and even business lunches (what business lunches?) because a) I find lunch completely fucks up one's day, especially when one's day begins shortly before a normal lunch hour, and b) because I'm never up in time, so can't anyway – but I had a sudden longing to have lunch with Harold, as we'd used to regularly, when we were youngish men, fit and able – able for what? well, lunch in my case . . .

FOR AND AGAINST OBLIVION

I went out. Had just read Ian Hamilton's posthumous book which arrived yesterday, read it last night and then much of it again this morning – it's called *Against Oblivion*, and it's a sort of version of Johnson's *Lives of the Poets*, at least Johnson's *Lives of the Poets* was his model, the point from which he began. It consists of short essays, four or five pages long, on twentieth-century poets, all of whom have to meet two qualifications – one, that they are dead; two, that they either wrote a few, in some cases only two or three poems (in Gregory Corso's case only one) that in Ian's view are good enough to be preserved from oblivion, or represent some fashion in the narrative of the century's poetry that ought to be placed on record. It's upsetting to read, this last book of Ian's, which he worked on almost to the day of his death and which he spoke about often during his illness – his desperation to get it finished, the last thing of that kind – by which he meant prose studies, critical essays, literary journalism, the higher hack work, *that* kind is what he meant when he said the last thing of *that* kind he'd ever do – when he finished it he was going to retire, not give a fuck any more about any of it, read for pleasure, for pleasure only, watch television, football, and hope that poems, or the beginning of poems, might arrive, to grow into all the writing he ever wanted to do ever again –

And I would think, as he spoke like this, that he was running his own race against oblivion, not the oblivion of a neglectful posterity, but his own oblivion, very personal, out of the here and now and into nowhere that makes any sense, viewed at least from the here and now –

Well, of course, Wittgenstein said – what was it precisely – 'Of those things of which we cannot speak, let us be silent' – and I've seen it in another formulation, or is it translation, 'thereof' or was it 'whereof we cannot speak, let us be silent', so let's try it this way, if you want, 'whereof and thereof we must be silent, let us not speak' – there it is, then, finally unravelled, or should it perhaps be ravelled, into perfect meaninglessness because look, look here, if you can't speak of something, whether it's thereof or whereof, then you will be silent, tautologically silent, so to speak, about that something – and if the something whereof or thereof is death, as repute hath it (but how can we know?), then not only will we speak about it, we will in fact insist on speaking about it, because we cannot in fact not speak about it, it does vex us so – well, well, I mean by this, when I think of the manner of Ian's dying, of his having died, and what his absence has done, is doing, to my life, I find myself wishing to speak of it, endlessly, even though I haven't the language for it – there is Tennyson's phrase, it must be from *In Memoriam*, death of Hallam, was it? – when it comes to it I only remember the last few words, it's when he's writing about how to write about death, Hallam's death, and finds he has no language for it, 'no language but a cry', which is really the point, except it's the poet's business to provide a language for the cry, which Tennyson does in those five words – perhaps not in *In Memoriam*, come to think of it, perhaps from somewhere else, but it's certainly Tennyson. In my view.

A LITTLE OUTING

So having read Ian's book again, I went out this afternoon, with nowhere to go, not at all, but with my OAP bus pass to take me there absolutely free. I ended up on Queensway. I always end up on Queensway these days – sometimes I set forth with the intention of travelling far afield, abroad so to speak – well, Queensway is abroad, a heady place to be at my age, like walking along the pavement of eighteen foreign countries, every overheard word a foreign one. I went into the ice-skating palace, sat on a stool watching the skaters for a while, and then went into that enormous shop, Whiteleys, up to their cinema complex. I bought a ticket for one of the films, but I didn't plan to go to it. Instead I bought a hot dog and a coffee and a diet coke (undrinkable, as it came from a tap, not a bottle) and went upstairs to the cinema bar, closed in the afternoons, but the tables are there, and you can sit at them – there are only two proper tables, as a matter of fact, but they were both unoccupied, so I settled at the one that's in front of a large cardboard cut-out of Alfred Hitchcock from where you can peer over the balcony railing down to the ground floor and watch people passing each other with their packages and their prams, but best of all this afternoon, I could watch the children on the trampoline, bouncing higher and higher, really very high they bounced, some with their faces turned up in joy at the height they got to, others keeping their heads down, concentrating on getting higher yet – it was lovely to see them at it, as I ate my hot dog, sipped my coffee, smoked my cigarettes. I stayed there for about an hour, then went back to Queensway, walked to Bayswater, and got the bus home. The conductor didn't bother to glance at my freedom pass when I proffered it to him, my face and baggy figure being enough to tell the story of my age, my right to a free journey,

I suppose. It would be nice if they were taught to study the card, check out the photograph with a slight air of suspicion, just to humour us.

VANISHING POETS

But why did I have to go out? Was it too much, too soon, of Ian's voice, as if the book bore the absence down on one more completely – but the book isn't the man, the style isn't the man, otherwise who would need the man when they have a book so completely of Ian's style as this, his last one, possibly his best book in that it goes beyond the usual style, without losing all the usual, the celebrated Ian Hamilton wit, clarity, urbanity, etc. – and each essay, each of the forty-five is a model of coherence without making each life into a coherence in itself. Something is left unexplained, unformulated but suggested – is that true, or do I just want it to be true? We did once spend a whole dinner discussing whether he hadn't always played it a bit safe in his writing, the Hamilton seated at the desk too aware of the Hamilton standing at his shoulder keeping a watch for any hint of vagueness, softness of feeling, looseness of expression, so that rigour, urbanity, wit became the whole bill of goods in itself, that we got Ian's intellectual virtues without actually ever quite getting Ian – well, did we want all of Ian in his biographies, which were after all not about him but about Robert Lowell, Matthew Arnold, J.D. Salinger – though towards the end of the life of Robert Lowell you can feel all Ian's unwritten revulsion working its way through the prose – besides, whose business was it but Ian's to decide how much of himself he should give to the world in his writing, just be grateful that you had so much of the man himself for so many years –

One of the essays is on a poet called – hang on – Weldon Kees, the only poet in the book I've never heard of, but it's not because of that, my lack of acquaintance with his work and even his name that I don't quite believe in him, the story Ian gives us of this Weldon Kees, that one day at the age of forty-one he left his car in a car park near San Francisco's Golden Gate Bridge and vanished, nobody knows whether he killed himself or exchanged his way of life for another way of life or what – but he was, according to Ian, a bitter poet, almost, now and then, but never quite celebrated – my own story exactly, but here I am, not only unvanished but physically, lumpishly available – yes, but then you're not Weldon Kees, are you? But then was Weldon Kees Weldon Kees, or is he a representative of a certain period in literary history, that it amused Ian to fictionalize for us? Ian gives us no hard information, no personal history at all, or at least nothing sufficiently particular, though there's an appearance of the particular, of detail, in the study, you can't actually find a fact to hang your concentration on, the whole essay slips through without quite sticking, so when you've finished it you find yourself wondering what it is you've read, and even find yourself checking for further information – the man in the small photograph above the essay looks rather like the young Orson Welles, by the way, but we can't see his face clearly as his head is bent over a newspaper, a Citizen Kane hat pushed rakishly to the back of his head – so even the photograph has a bogus look to it, and no source is given for it, while sources seem to be given for all the other poets' photographs.

As for Weldon Kees's poems, the two Ian publishes feature a kind of poetical-functional character called Robinson, a wispy offshoot of Prufrock, and like Ian's essay in that you can't quite grasp him, can't quite grasp the images – I read them several times, then shut my eyes and tried to remember what I'd only just read, and really nothing came back but a rather diluted tone, portentously calm – flat, really – with a pseudo-not-quite-phoney, phoney would be too concrete a word, so yes, pseudo-plangency – I mean, why would a writer try to make a career out of such unvividly expressed life that really only succeeds in suggesting unvividly lived life – or could that be the point of the poetry? – and if so, how could that be a point worth publishing? – unless we're meant to see it as in some way symptomatic of the nature of Ian's activity in the book – look, he might be saying, here are all these real lives, real poems, and here, slipped in amongst them, is an imitation of both, does it really matter if we don't notice the difference because how can such a procedure give us the truth? may be the question Ian is satirically asking of himself, as well as of us, by inventing Weldon Kees. If Weldon Kees is an invention. Suppose he actually existed – might still exist, now in his eighties, alive in some corner of a foreign field – Uxbridge, for instance? – in which case everything I've written down is nonsense except, I suppose, the central point, which is that I don't believe in Ian's Weldon Kees, whether he existed, still exists, or not –

I suppose what I miss from the book, churlishly, is an essay like Dr Johnson's on Savage – of course, Johnson knew Savage, had strong feelings about him, his family – mother, especially – the way he'd been treated, his madness – there is Savage brought before you with vigorous pity and some pain – well, why should Ian have tried the same? and well, why not? He knew Lowell, had met him a number of times over the years, knew many of his friends, wives, mistresses, etc. and once asked me to join Lowell and him for dinner, actually pressed me because he couldn't face doing it on his own – an evening with Lowell could be slightly tricky and somewhat exhausting, Ian said, especially when he was on medication for his psychiatric problems, which he currently was –

he (Ian) needed moral support, and what's more I should welcome the chance to pay my respects to a poet I admired, eh? – well, I said, it's true that I admired some of the poems, especially 'Home After Nine Months Away', but I wasn't sure I admired enough of them to spend a tricky and exhausting evening – Oh, come on! he said, I'm paying! It took place at L'Epicure, in Soho, where Ian and I lunched in those days, we had become good friends with the owner, his wife, and the two waiters, and it was probably the place in London we felt most at home in when we weren't at home – in fact Ian's affairs were such at that time that he probably felt more at home there than at home, often when I left late in the afternoon he'd stay on at the table in his leather armchair – luxurious seating was one of the tiny restaurant's many charms – as if intending to elide his post-lunch brandy into a pre-dinner Scotch. We arranged to meet at 7.30, Lowell having told Ian he would turn up at eight. By nine o'clock or so the evening was going well, very well, in the usual way – 'Perhaps he won't turn up,' Ian said hopefully, but an hour later he did, delivered by a middle-aged, plain-looking woman who went away again immediately. What followed was pretty ghastly – well, how could it not be, as he was full of psychiatric drugs, and soon of alcohol – it was distressing to see this ruined poet with his noble, slightly hydrocephalic head lolling, uttering slurred and muddled sentences accompanied by mumbling laughter, even drooling a little – once or twice there was an odd gleam in his otherwise befuddled eyes, that looked very like malice – as when he asked Ian to order up yet another plate of oysters, which he covered with pepper and sauces but didn't eat, and a further bottle of wine when there were still two half-drunk on the table, and Ian, whose financial situation was dire, began to look anxious. I was sure that Lowell took this in, and savoured it, but when the middle-aged woman returned to collect him, he suddenly became alert, told Ian he wanted to pay his share of the bill, studied it carefully, wrote out a cheque, handed it to Ian with the sweetest and most gracious of smiles, shook him by the hand, shook me by the hand, thanked us both for the pleasant evening, put his arm through the lady's, and left. 'Well,' I said, for lack of anything better, 'at least he paid his way.' 'More than paid his way,' Ian said, showing me the cheque, which was made out to a scrawl, and signed by a scrawl, and was for the sum of six million dollars, or thereabouts.

Now I'm not saying that in the essay in *Against Oblivion* Ian should have given us Lowell as he presented himself that evening, but you wouldn't think, from reading it, that he'd ever met him, he's so superbly encompassed by Ian's prose – one of the reasons one always remembers Johnson on Pope is Johnson's own tenderness in reflecting on Pope's love of his parents – and his description of Pope's personal appearance – the description of his getting up in the morning and dressing – the tininess of his body, his little dress sword, his walking in the garden practising his numbers, talking to himself in couplets – Johnson makes us see Pope without Johnson, using a prose that only Johnson could have written, while Ian makes us understand and judge Lowell only as Ian does – no room to manoeuvre, really – you have the feeling that if you don't agree with Ian's understanding and judgement, then likely you're being stupid, phoney or sniffing a whiff of faction that'll lead you to wilful misjudgement – in almost every one of Ian's essays there is a glimpse of the literary pond life, in which there seems to be a ceaseless activity – literary careers, poetic careers, in the making and the breaking – and why should one be surprised and disgusted by it, one only has to read one's Dryden, one's Pope, one's Ben Jonson all the way back to Shakespeare, and Greene, etc. to know that it's always been going on, perhaps right on back to the

knowable beginnings, with the juries at the Greek festivals being
fixed for Sophocles, Aeschylus, and against Euripides – in with the
wrong crowd, weak, no political muscle, poor PR – but those were
real careers, bringing real fame, a fame that's endured two or three
thousand years, but surely Lowell, aiming for the top, could only
have expected to remain at the top for what? fifty, sixty, seventy
years after his death, and Ian's essay, where he's far less admiring of
the poetry than he is in the biography, will shake him a bit from the
top, down a branch or two, and maybe he'll only get thirty, forty
years of posthumous fame, let's hope he enjoys them.

I'm trying to make my way back out of all this, to when I left the
house after reading *Against Oblivion* – I didn't want to think about
the book, or Ian, whom I can see now, by the way, whenever I lift
my eyes to the window sill, there he is in a photograph not taken by
me, when I first knew him in his late twenties his teeth were broken
and discoloured, and although he had them fixed at various stages
in his life, so that they looked for long stretches rather magnificent
really, he kept the habit of smiling in such a way that he never
revealed his teeth, which is why it was, in effect, always a toothless
grin – but in this photograph he is as I best remember him, the grin
has a sound to it if you know the grin, a laugh heaving up from deep
inside him, that when it broke through, took hold of the upper body
and shook it from side to side and backwards and forwards, he
would subside into coughing, momentary exhaustion, some slightly
surprised smiling and blinking, and then would often start again –

ON THE INTERNET AT LAST!

Bound and Gagged in Montreal, is where I left myself a long way
back, at the age of six or was it seven? The story unfinished and

actually unstarted, although it was one of the most significant events in my life. I can't seem to get into it, perhaps because I actually don't seem to know much about it except the event itself – there were the nuns, of course, who have suddenly popped up, but the nuns didn't have anything to do with it, God knows really where they came from or who they belonged to, perhaps they were roving the streets hoping to happen on a small, easily led gang like ourselves – Nigel and I, two other boys, not Carole, this was a boys only sort of business – so four boys being led by the three nuns down Vendôme Avenue, and then along some other streets into a house, down a hall into a room in which there was a table on which there was a dead boy. He was dressed in a suit, his hair was shiny and slicked back, his cheeks were pink and powdery. One of the nuns said he had been killed while riding on his bicycle. He had grabbed the back of a truck, had been pulled along faster and faster and faster, the truck stopped suddenly, he had smashed into the back. Here we saw the consequences of such behaviour. We must look at him properly so that we would remember him whenever we were riding our bicycles, and so wouldn't cling to the backs of trucks, would we? We said we wouldn't. We didn't say we couldn't because we didn't have bicycles. The three nuns led us out of the house, and went back inside. We went home. It was like a dream then, and is like a dream now, and I'm only sure it happened because I've checked with Nigel, who remembers it as clearly as I do – more clearly, as he remembers that one of the nuns wore spectacles. But it was something else in Montreal, not bound and gagged there.

But here's a thing, here's a thing might help. I've just got myself on to the Internet, or rather, as I've been on it for years, I've just discovered how to use it. Some chap that Victoria knows, who does all her computer tasks for her – and for me too, apparently, though

I wasn't really aware of it – his name is Steve, and it's true that I've seen him around the house, coming up from the basement or out of her study, and sometimes he's come into my study, fiddled around briefly on the computer and gone out again, I haven't yet seen him coming out of our bedroom, but then why would he go in there, as there's no computer there? – anyway, he's a handsome chap, neatly put together, with astonishing violet eyes, and a quiet, gentle-but-firm-and-clear-minded manner, and a strange little pouch that looks almost like a cache-sexe, except that it hangs outside his trousers – anyway, this chap Steve turned up yesterday at 2 p.m., when I was bound to be up and about, and left half an hour later, having taught me how to use the Internet – half an hour is all it took him to teach me something that I'd never tried to learn before because I was sure I'd never master it, and there I was, another half an hour later, 'browsing the Internet', getting my search system, called Google, up on the screen, and trying out a couple of names, of two playwriting friends of mine, and up came information about both of them. In each case I surfaced in the middle of rather unpleasant reviews of their plays, so I decided there and then, on the spot, that I would under no circumstances ever visit my own name – I haven't learnt how to browse the Internet in order to browse through bad reviews, which I make such a point of avoiding in real life, and so I sat for a while trying to work out in which pasture I really wanted to browse and graze, and it came to me, with a thrill, a thrill at the thought of it, but without much hope, but anyway into the box I tapped the name Hank Janson – and there it was. He was. A whole thingamabob, website, website devoted to Hank Janson, with little rectangles marking history, background, character, books, author, etc. – I placed my little cursor on books, and there they were, on the left-hand side small copies of the covers – all the covers – and on the right-hand side plot summaries and critiques – I went straight for the covers, putting my arrow on a small cover and pressing. I got an enlargement of the first Hank Janson cover I'd ever seen, *Sister, Don't Hate Me* – the title I'd forgotten, the cover unforgettable, a young blonde, gag around her mouth, hands bound behind her back, stocking legs tucked under her, her face turned towards us, the large blue eyes innocent and alarmed, a curl of hair tumbling over a mildly troubled forehead – talk about madeleines – hah! – I really went through the most astonishing tumble of emotions, the confusion of desire and thrilled shame, the twelve-and-a-half-year-old standing at the bookstall beside Leicester Square station, and yet what was I, actually, as I experienced all that, all those years shed, what was I but a man of sixty-five, bent mournfully and salaciously over his computer, or thus I believed I would have appeared to anyone looking through the window, if that anyone had been me – but if it had been somebody else, Victoria, for instance, Victoria, yes, Victoria would have seen her elderly husband toiling at his work as ever, not that she could have seen me through the window anyway, at least without standing on a ladder, as my room is at the top of the house, or where the top of the house was before we added an attic, so forget Victoria standing on a ladder looking in on me through the window, come back to the simple double-image, a twelve-and-a-half-year-old staring, wet-kneed, at the bound and captive blonde on the cover of *Sister, Don't Hate Me* on an open bookstall near Leicester Square station, a sixty-five-year-old sitting in his study under the attic staring at the same cover, etc. – almost the first time since I was an adult that I've been able to short-circuit myself back, back beyond twelve and a half, all the way back to an afternoon in Montreal. I am sitting on a chair facing the class, my hands tied behind my back, my ankles tied to the legs of the chair. I was in my first week or so of school, so I was six years old, and I was crying and making a terrible fuss, obviously, which was why the teacher had tied a handkerchief around my mouth to stop me interrupting the class. Someone came in, an adult, a woman, looked at me with disgust – so it seemed to me, but it might have been shock or anger – and gave the teacher a piece of paper, a message, I suppose, and went out. Now that is all I remember. I know the teacher was a woman, but not how old she was, nor what she looked like – I have an impression of spectacles, large spectacles, but it's only an impression, and I have no idea what led up to this punishment, which I suppose it to have been, though for all I know the teacher might have been acting on an erotic impulse, or may have been anti-English, but I assume there was a motive that led to it – I have a suspicion that I was considered a chatterbox and disruptive, although the truth is that I spent my first year at school in Montreal, for pretty well the whole of it, in a state of terror – the Englishness of me constituting a continuous offence among my peer group. This was, no doubt, the worst period of my childhood, and so probably of my life – they would ambush me on the way to and from school, administer a beating, throw my bag and cap into snow banks in the winter, through the open windows of unknown houses in the summer, lock me in garages, in fact pretty mundane stuff as the world now goes. Now where was Nigel in all this, how did he avoid this daily ghastliness, because I think he did avoid it, I have a sense of him as being at ease in his schooldays – although of course his began a year before mine, he may have gone through it all while I was still a favoured stay-at-home, snug in Grandma's arms or bed, but I don't believe he did. I must ask him the next time we have an evening together. On the other hand, how much do I really want to recall of that time? Perhaps I should go to a shrink, get some of this buried state unburied. I might discover the why of my being tied down by my teacher, but then why bother, the point of living beyond one's childhood is that it all happened back there, whatever good or ill happened happened back there. It's not as if we have to live with the consequences in any way that makes sense. Only psychiatrists who believe in clear logical paths between past and present, unconscious and conscious, can believe that at sixty-five I continue to live with the consequences of what the monstrous woman, whom I only think of as monstrous for this single act, it may have been the monstrous lapse of a mainly kindly soul – and I mustn't forget that I was an exceptionally pretty child, quite gorgeous, in fact, if early photographs are anything to go by (and remained so until my early teens, when my nose suddenly put on a spurt) and possibly I was to her as the girl on the cover of *Sister, Don't Hate Me* was to me only six years later – I mean, on the one hand a succulent little moppet with an English accent, what more delicious than to bind and gag him and put him on public display, on the other a succulent blonde with heaving breasts, what more delicious than to bind and gag her and have her on the cover of a book which you have in your pocket for a mere one shilling and sixpence – but a mere one and six was hard to come by when my pocket money was two shillings a week.

Hence my career in crime.

I've just looked Weldon Kees up on the Internet. He existed. Perhaps still does, somewhere.

A THING AND OTHER THINGS

Here's a thing. A drizzly afternoon. I woke to it shortly after midday, with the house empty – a note from Victoria reporting that she'd be out to lunch, there was no sign of George so assumed she'd gone off with her walker, no sign of Tom, in fact the only living creature to be found was Errol, who in fact evinced few signs of life, he was curled into a thick ball on the sofa, his tail wrapped around him, so at first glance you would have mistaken him for a woollen cushion. I gave him a little poke, said a few words, to make sure he was OK, and he gave one of his mousy little squeaks, otherwise didn't stir, even when I went into the kitchen to make breakfast – usually I can't shake him off my heels when I go to the kitchen, he assumes that he eats when I eat, stands on his hind legs with his front legs whirring until I pop something into his mouth – then I came up here, thinking that I really must get on with a play I'm writing about some English people marooned on a Greek island. I've been stuck for ages in a scene where people keep on talking but I can't make out why I have them saying what they're saying, I don't know what they want, and when I don't know what characters want I don't know who they are, and how they've got onto the page – I sat looking at a line of dialogue – PRYNNE: You would say that, wouldn't you! – which began to incense me, as the line that provokes this, from a character currently called HENRIETTA, is completely inert, idle speaking to fill the silence, idle writing to fill the space – so then I thought I might as well get on with this for a while, but the thought of the last sentence – 'Hence my career in crime' – depressed me, I felt no stirrings of either guilt or joy at the prospect of remembering my career in crime, so I went to the window, stared out at the drizzle, wondering who would want to go out in that who didn't have to, and went out in it, though I didn't have to – or perhaps I did, who knows? I tramped up Holland Park, past the bus stop, aimless but conscious of my hair getting matty from the wet, wishing I still had my Russian-style, waterproof hat that I lost or was stolen from me last year, then heard – no felt – a bus coming up behind me. I got back to the stop and clambered aboard before it could pull away, promising myself that for once I'd ride it all the way to Oxford Circus, but got off at Queensway as usual, went into the ice rink. There was nobody skating. Nobody. Back into Queensway, where there were quite a few people all right, but not milling about as they usually are, coming towards you in groups talking excitedly in foreign tongues, they seemed listless, as if they didn't really have any business or pleasure in mind, like me they were out because they didn't want to be in, but they didn't want to be out either. Much the same feeling in Whiteleys, where I bought a hot dog, a diet coke and a ticket to *Harry Potter*, and went up to the bar. I hoped briefly that I'd go into the film, but I was sure the cinema would be empty, or almost so, and the vision of myself sitting alone in a cinema on a Tuesday afternoon, watching a film about a child with large spectacles doing magic and defeating wizards and battling dragons in a prep school, which is I gather what he does, struck me as so pathetic. When I was at Cambridge, an undergraduate, alone in the cinema apart from a type like me as I am now, I would try to imagine his life, the hopelessness and uselessness of it, the squalor and pathos, etc., and now, of course, I imagined there'd be someone of twenty-two or so in to see *Harry Potter* who would try to imagine the squalor and pathos of my life, etc., so really I thought I'd be better at the bar, looking over the rail and watching the young bouncing on the trampoline – actually I knew that it would be like the ice rink, nobody would be on the trampolines, nobody, but at least there'd be the shoppers, the prams and pushchairs, little packs of Muslims, Japanese – but when I lit my cigarette, drew my chair over to the rail and looked down it wasn't just that there was nobody on the trampolines, which I'd expected, or that there weren't any trampolines, which I'd half-expected, as they'd obviously been temporary, but – and here's the thing – below the bar, where I'd remembered trampolines, were escalators – escalators that had been there since I'd first come to Whiteleys, on which I'd often ascended and descended, on which, indeed, I'd just ascended to get to the cinema complex. So what had happened the other afternoon, when I'd seen the children bouncing? Had I sat at the table, stared down at the elevators, and hallucinated trampolines instead, a reasonable enough replacement when you think about it, after all most of us would far rather trampoline up and down a shopping mall than trundle through it on escalators – I suppose I'd seen the trampolines somewhere else in Whiteleys, and when I got home and wrote it down I conflated the memory of sitting at the table, looking down, with the memory of the trampolines – after all, the escalators were so familiar I wouldn't have noticed them in memory. But supposing there weren't any trampolines in Whiteleys, and never have been, then I'm dealing with a real hallucination – well, certainly much better than my usual hallucinations – I'll ask Victoria when she gets back, I have the distinct impression that I mentioned the trampolines to her, and that she said she'd seen them too, weren't they delightful – but what if she says she hadn't seen them, as far as she knew there had never been trampolines in Whiteleys, what a preposterous thought, trampolines in Whiteleys – perhaps better not to ask her. Better to go on with PRYNNE: You would say that, wouldn't you! – or my career in crime. One or the other. Which?

CRIME

It began with fairly rhapsodic pilfering from Daddy's trouser pocket and Mummy's purse – no skill required for either, I collected money from his trousers every morning for my tube or bus fare, he lay in bed with his tea, papers and post, his trousers lay over the back of a chair, I said from the bedroom door, 'Can I have my fare please,' he gestured to his trousers, and I took out the shilling or whatever and palmed an extra coin or two – and Mummy's purse was always to be found in her handbag which was likely to be found anywhere, and quite often when she wasn't near it. I moved from this rhapsodic pilfering to a more organized and rewarding level entirely by accident, when an aunt chose, for reasons inexplicable, to give me a Georgian penny for a birthday present – inexplicable as I had never shown or had the slightest interest in old coins but of course perfectly explicable if you know that the aunt in question was a pretty mean old bird, who probably turned up the forgotten coin in a drawer, and always one to make do, made it do as a birthday present to her nephew – who carried it around in his pocket for days, hoping that he might find a use for it, and eventually did. I was with my two closest friends at school, one called Quass, and the other Eddis. Quass was short and Jewish, with a terrible sideways grin that he had difficulty removing, especially when he was in trouble; Eddis was a lanky, blond, sardonic boy, who was an exotic in that his parents were divorced, he lived with his mother, and his father now and then turned up at school, an elegant man, soldierly, and drunk. We constituted a small gang of outsiders, really, the three of us in the lowest form in the school, Transitus C, contemptuous of work because we were brighter than the rest of the form. Idle and jeering, we were capable of making each other laugh to the point of physical collapse – really it was the jeering strain that bound us closely, nothing and nobody in the school commanded our respect, especially anything we didn't understand or anyone we suspected of being gifted and intelligent – our conversation reduced the world to our level, or just beneath it, as we had, needless to say, no respect for each other – but that was justified, as we knew each other so well. *Folie à trois.*

Folie à trois. We were at St James's Park tube station, late afternoon, going home, I suppose – Quass lived in Dolphin Square, Eddis in Queen's Elm Gardens, now why should I remember that when I don't recall some of my own addresses, the street that I lived on for nearly a year in Vancouver, for instance, although I remember the desk against the window, through a corner of which I could see the sea, and through which I could also, if I looked down at certain times of the evening, see the parked car in which sat the large, handsome wife of a small handsome colleague. She was in love with me, was the only explanation I could offer myself for her parking there, as I typed steadily away on my second novel, occasionally glancing down at her – I never went down to ask what she was doing or would she like to come in, and she never rang the bell – after a time she'd drive off, and I'd have a sense of mild relief, and absolutely no sense of an opportunity missed, although I liked her very much, as much as I liked her husband – every Saturday night the three of us would meet up, along with several other colleagues of the English Department at the University of British Columbia in Vancouver's China town and have a festive dinner – nothing in her manner on those occasions suggested she was in love with me, but I expect, if she's still alive, she would still remember my address. I don't remember it in an absolutely complete sense, as if I hadn't really known it even while I was living there, and yet for over half a century Eddis's and Quass's addresses have been lodged in me, addresses I visited – well, twice for tea with Eddis and his mother, Mrs Eddis (he spoke to her with the cool contempt of an estranged husband, from whom he'd probably learnt it), and only once to the Quasses, for a legal briefing – but let us suppose then that we were at St James's Park tube for the purposes of going home, Quass to Victoria, Eddis for South Kensington, I for Sloane Square, and while we were sorting through our pockets for money to put in the ticket machine – this is how it happened – I found the aunt's Georgian coin, offered it to Quass and Eddis in exchange for real money, say twopence, was jeeringly rejected, and then one of us, the one of us with the sharpest eye for an improbable chance – not me, more probably Eddis – popped it into the two-shilling slot of the sixpence-halfpenny ticket machine. It fell through the various runners, runners and channels, and landed with a chink and a clump, falling, we realized, into a pile of other coins, accepted coins. This was going to be a familiar sound over the coming weeks, months, a sound deeply satisfying, deeply ominous, the clink and the clump of immediate wealth, impending disaster. I never believed we wouldn't be caught in the end, so the usual criminal's prayer, adapted from St Augustine, not this time, please, God – don't let it be *this* time – anyway, after a moment spent taking in the full meaning of that noise, that clink and that clump, one of us put in a halfpenny, and the machine stuttered, and it trembled and heaved, and out popped the sixpence-halfpenny ticket, and one and sixpence – in the form of three sixpences – change. The machine, in other words, had received the Georgian penny as if it were a modern (1949) florin. So we had sixpence each. The next step, which we took immediately – or so it seems in memory, though there must have been some working out, some research – we found a numismatist around the corner from the Hank Janson bookstall, where we discovered that Georgian pennies were two a penny – well, actually one for twopence. So, we could buy a Georgian penny for twopence, put the Georgian penny in the two-shilling slot of the sixpence-halfpenny ticket machine, a halfpenny in the halfpenny slot, and in return would receive a sixpence-halfpenny ticket, and three sixpences (one shilling and sixpence) in change – along, of course with a sixpence-halfpenny tube ticket, which for some reason we couldn't use, perhaps because we were under sixteen and had to travel on half fares that were actually marked across the ticket (I have a memory of two red stripes?), and travelling on an adult ticket would have raised suspicion – or perhaps we regarded the tickets as evidence that had to be disposed of. But even if we failed to maximize our profits, they rapidly became so vast that we couldn't keep up with them – you have to keep in mind that one, just one, Georgian coin and a halfpenny bought a whole Hank Janson – the London Underground was, in fact, financing my masturbation, was also financing as much of the fraudulent cherried cakes, ice creams, etc. as I could eat, and there were still handfuls – by the time we were caught twenty pounds' worth – of sixpences under the floorboard where I kept *Hotsie, You'll be Chilled, Lola Brought Her Wreath*, both genuine titles, I've just checked on Hank's website. Heady days, those were, and full of terror. The accumulation of sixpences became more addictive than the addictions I was feeding them to (buns, cinemas, Jansons) – I say 'I' here because I don't know what Quass and Eddis spent their money on – both bought Hank Jansons, but not as needily as I did, I think, and we didn't really discuss our sexual habits, practices, predilections, whichever word would be appropriate. Eddis maintained a rather aloof attitude to such matters, anyway, kept his council, Quass and I would have possibly a brief, excited but careful conversation about which ones we'd read – but in textual terms – 'You know, the one where he's escaping from the gangsters' – and never really in terms of the true story, which was there, undismissably on the cover and came up in the narrative only as incidents. In fact, our conversations, inasmuch as we had them, were not unlike the careful, thoughtful plods through the texts, as they explicitly call them, on the website – we have the plots of *Hotsie, You'll be Chilled*, etc. with all the 'incidents' ignored, apart from an occasional en passant reference, *regretful* reference to H.J.'s tendency to roughness with women, but the nature, the style, the dash and panache of that 'roughness' is excluded, in the oddly brutish and punitively puritanical, not to say verbally genteel, age we live in – so we have the plots, a meticulous rundown on the main characters, some esoteric snatches of comparative analysis, i.e. 'though *Torment For Trixie* lacks the range and scope of the narrative of the earlier *Frails Can Be So Tough*' etc. – and even pernickety observations on H.J.'s sudden changes of style and tone within the texts, the whole purpose and point of the man and his writing is not so much lost as wilfully and insultingly slighted – but there, lying beside these turgid and earnest critiques lie the heart of the matter in the reproduced covers. I can't say that Quass and I managed to conduct our discourse at the same level as the discourses on the website, but in common with the website we talked around what mattered most to us – at least so I assume, of course for Quass it may have been the plot, characters, narrative style, etc. all along.

A NIGHT OUT

I'd never heard it played straight through before, though I recognized bits and pieces as they came up, the Shepherds' Farewell at the beginning of the second part, for instance, and the later choral passages, especially the last, which seemed to me astounding, and the choir itself – I've never experienced quite such a gorgeous hushing, the noise seeming to fade slowly, so slowly, right inside oneself – but actually, being neither musical nor religious (at the moment) I couldn't make any real sense of the whole – none of these passages of beautiful music seemed to move into the next part or grow out of the last, each passage just happened independently, in spite of programme notes and translations of the songs that suggested that this was a structured telling of the story of Christ's childhood. Actually, it becomes a very peculiar, very sentimental story, if you take God out of it, which is what I think Berlioz did – how else explain the Shepherds' wish that Christ 'grow and prosper/ And be a good father in his turn,' seeming to mean, not a spiritual Father, but a biological father. Had Berlioz thought this through, one wonders, or did he intend a piercing reference to what was missing from Christ's life, or had he merely forgotten the theological facts – but I came out feeling reverential, though possibly it was a reverence for the genius in the music – a genius that expressed itself for an hour and three quarters without a break – I could scarcely believe it, though I checked on Victoria's watch too – an hour and three quarters in the theatre is for me unendurable – physically unendurable, the need for a pee, the need for a cigarette, the need to stand up, walk, stretch etc. would have overpowered my concentration for the last half-hour at least, but not at *L'Enfance du Christ.* We seemed to waft out of the auditorium, at least until our feet hit the bizarre undulating floor of the Barbican – the only floor I've come across that makes you seasick just to walk a few paces on – why did they do it, whoever did it, in fact why did they do the Barbican at all, unless as a challenge to the seriousness of the audience's intentions – the concrete wastes that surround the building, the tunnel that leads to the building, the hideousness of the building itself, make you feel that you've entered a war zone, the final bunker – and then inside, the vast undulating floor, with double and triple sofas arbitrarily arranged by way of seating. On Saturday evening one small area had been roped off, to make a sort of pen in which some elderly people were sitting side by side or at angles to each other, as if they were in quarantine, or petitioners for a stay of execution. They were quite still, not talking, and there was a placard swinging over their heads, on which was written 'Friends of the LSO'.

We went on to dinner in the West End. London was London on a Saturday night, Hogarth or Hieronymus Bosch, take your pick – in the restaurant we bumped into several people we knew, actors and two playwrights, so there was a lot of kissing, the women kissing the women, the men kissing the women, and muddled into all this, the men kissing the men – some of us were heterosexual, but still we ran into each other's arms, rubbed cheeks, kissed, as we made growling sounds of pleasure and love – this male cuddling is a new fashion, probably come over from New York or Russia, and I don't really like it, really rather hate it, especially when they have beards, like both of the playwrights and one of the actors, they're rough on my skin, and probably full of food and insects, and they're smelly, but I see no way of repelling them unless I take to dribbling into them or blowing my nose over them, and word gets round that I'm to be avoided, however soft-skinned, clean and inviting my own cheeks are. I'd had the wit to book a quiet table, so we settled to a good meal and talked about the Berlioz, and then about our writing problems, and over coffee I told Victoria that she looked beautiful, which she did, and how happy she makes me, which she does. She thought about this, and then asked me what was I up to, what was the matter, what had I done? – her usual response when I pay her a compliment, and the reason that I don't pay her more. 'Well,' I said, 'well –' then as if changing the subject, 'Do you remember the trampolines in Whiteleys, a few weeks ago?' 'Oh yes,' she said, 'all those children bouncing, wasn't it lovely?' So that was all right then. When we got home we threw the tennis ball around the front hall for George for a while, and then went to our studies, I to write this, she to work on her stories, though I could hear the ball bouncing, George barking, Victoria laughing.

THE MEANING OF PLOP

Victoria Station was our favourite haunt, a junction into which we could tube from our different places of residence, make a quick killing, then on together to school. It was also special in that its sixpence-halfpenny machine never failed to deliver, accepting warped and wafer-thin Georgian pennies that the machines in other stations rejected with embarrassingly loud groans and grating sounds. It was in the middle of a line of five machines, I think. Yes, five. The backs of five other machines were lined up directly opposite, about a yard away, and there was a machine at the end of the double line, each facing out, thus creating a rectangle of ticket machines, with an inner rectangle of space, which an underground employee could step into by pulling aside one of the machines at the end. He could then open the backs of the machines to collect the coins, put in a new pack of tickets, adjust whatever mechanics needed adjusting – very efficiently organized, I now see, making it easy for a policeman, for instance, to enter the inner rectangle, open the back of the 6d½ machine, crouch down out of sight, cup his hand under the 2s runner and catch the penny as it fell – a legal necessity, because if the coin joined the heap already in the machine, it would be impossible to prove when and by whose hand it had been inserted. The first indication that something was slightly off, therefore, came when the dropping of the coin wasn't followed by chink and clunk, but by a soft plop – it was audible, the plop, like a physical sensation in one's system rather than as a distinct noise – and there was the explanation, in the form of an adult's head rising from behind the machine, and simultaneously hands belonging to a second adult male standing behind us clasping each of us, Quass and myself, by the elbow. We were quite merry, Quass and I, all the way to the police station, as were the two policemen, who were flatteringly full of admiration for our little scheme, forgiving us for their having to spend long periods of time crouching, knees bent, behind the machines, waiting for the wrong penny to drop. I don't think we really worked out what was going to happen when we got to the station, perhaps the conviviality returned us to earlier childhood, the sense that we'd taken part in a game, and lost, with laughter all round, perhaps we were playing being jolly good losers, or perhaps it was minute by minute bravado, the mind refusing to progress even to the immediate consequences – but consequences became real at the station, when statements were taken down – confessions, I suppose they were – and most particularly when we had to give our names and addresses, and a telephone number where our parents could be reached – then the reality, reality of the situation, the pleadings not to call the parents, please, we won't do it again, we promise kind of thing – the Quass parents and the Gray parents turned up, I can't remember in what order, and I can't remember the journey home, or anything much apart from the shame and the fear and the moment when, hearing the mother approaching my room, I fell to my knees and assumed the praying posture, eyes closed. I heard the door open, and then heard the silence, as if the mother were joining me in this act of devotion. Then her voice, 'Oh, get up, you bloody little fool.' A day or so later, when we were walking together somewhere in Chelsea, after an eerie silence that had gone on virtually since she'd summoned me up from my knees, she said, her voice thick with emotion, 'I want you to know that your father and

I will always stand by you, whatever you do.' We walked some more. 'Because we know you'd never do anything like this again.' I can't remember whether I made a reply. Even now, I can't think what reply would have been the right one – although the honest one would have been a thank-you for the show of support, but a courteous refusal to guarantee that there wouldn't be a repeat – in fact, there were many repeats, though nothing on the scale of the slot machine swindle, nothing as imaginative, although occasionally, more shaming. At Cambridge I caught myself cheating at a poker game. I belonged to a Trinity poker school, we met twice, sometimes three times a week, played from about 9 p.m. to 3 a.m., and for – given our circumstances – quite high stakes, high enough for a loss to mean desperation, a gain a night out in London. One night, or early morning, on the last hand of the game – it was one of the very complicated games, either baseball or anaconda, with many cards on the table – I nudged, kind of nudged, one of those jerky little movements that I could almost pretend to myself was thoughtless, accidental – nudged a card one way, another card another way, thus giving myself a winning hand. I not only caught myself doing it but also caught myself pretending to myself that I wasn't. And there was a further self in me that took cool note of what the other two of me were up to – as did a Canadian, ten years older than the rest of us and much the best player, he also took note and noted aloud that he'd taken note, although choosing to pretend that what he'd taken note of was an accident – but I could tell from the gleam in his eyes that he saw me for what I was, not just a cheat but a cowardly cheat – I wonder if I could have gone through with it and accepted my winnings, or whether, not that honesty would have prevailed, whether my nerve would have failed, in other words, which was the stronger current in my nature, the cheating or the cowardly. I was never comfortable in that man's presence again, actually I'd never been comfortable in it before then, as I'd always thought there was something cynical and knowing about him, lacking somewhat in respect for his fellow men, particularly me, yes, that was possibly the worst of it, that I'd succeeded in confirming suspicions I knew he held about me.

I've just been out. I got as far as Holland Park Avenue, stepped on to the pavement, two screaming police cars hurtled towards where I was going to put my next step, lurched violently without breaking speed, screamed on in and out of traffic up the avenue – no doubt en route to a crime which will be completed, the perpetrators vanished, long before they've arrived with blood on their fenders and their warning siren still wailing – well, at least there's a good chance that they'll have something to show for their efforts, a broken or a dead body that supplies some of the material of a crime scene, even if they've provided it themselves – every time I read of them in the papers, or accounts of inquiries in which they are invariably acquitted of any offence, frequently saluted if not honoured and promoted for it, I feel ill with anger, in fact one day might come to be counted as one of their victims, though at long range, felled by a heart attack or an apoplexy induced by reading about them, as much their responsibility as if I'd been crushed under their wheels or bounced off their bonnets (hoods? what?) into the gutter. Anyway, I turned around and came home. I was out for about four minutes. It was enough.

PUNISHMENT

Quass wore his 'guilty as charged' grin, appropriately, as we were guilty as charged, but his grin also carried with it a different – entirely unintended, entirely inaccurate – message, not simply of guilt, but of gloating guilt, and I wished, for the first time in our relationship, as I stood with downcast eyes and hands clasped behind my back, that he'd wipe it off his face – whatever happened to him would happen to me, he was grinning and gloating for both of us. There were two men and a woman sitting at the desk before which we stood, one of whom must have been the magistrate – or perhaps they all were. They heard what we'd done from the policemen, and then asked us what we had to say. We said we were very sorry, it wouldn't happen again. Then my father spoke. He said he was very sorry, it wouldn't happen again. He then went on to speak of the career that lay before me, either promisingly or in ruins, depending on the judgement of the court – the terms in which he spoke of me, my achievements, my potential, the high moral regard in which I was held by form-master and housemaster, might have brought a blush to my cheek in other circumstances – but I can't imagine what they would have been, I really can't imagine any circumstances, except the one I was in, that would have prompted the father to have spoken so highly of me. He was usually as modest about me as he was about himself, although for different reasons, his modesty about himself being an acknowledged part of his charm, and doubtless contributing, along with his passivity (and for all I know, enormous cock), to his sexual success – anyway, the father spoke, the mother sat nobly beside him, possibly telling herself that she never thought she'd see the day when she'd see a son of hers, etc. When he sat down, Mr Quass rose, and spoke briefly to introduce his colleague who was sitting next to Mrs Quass. He was a grey-haired gentleman with a silver tongue, a barrister who specialized in criminal law (Mr Quass himself, I suddenly recall, specialized in maritime law), and in a speech of sonorous eloquence, in which he described Quass's and my future in such technicoloured terms that everyone in the court knew he was lying, nearly succeeded in destroying our lives. Well, my life. Well, my immediate future. But then who knows? Being sent to a remand school might have improved my future, if not immediately, at least by now – I could have been among the first of the 'redeemed' writers, a category I have only just invented, but I could have invented it back then, is my point, and would almost certainly have had less trouble getting my books published, my plays put on – a number of critics have long sneered at my typical English middle-class, public school and university educated, literary, so forth, so forth – a criminal record, reform school, where I would have learnt so much that is useful – robbery, buggery, etc. might have won me a respectful critical attention. Anyway, when Mr Quass's colleague sat down there was a revolted silence from a bench that had been previously disposed to take the policeman's view of the case, that we were decent little chaps who'd been unable to resist – what ordinary boy could have – the temptations that our natural intelligence, combined with an astonishingly unfortunate piece of good luck, had exposed us to. They stopped looking benevolent and scowled at me and most particularly at Quass, who of course gloated grinningly back at them – they put their heads together, muttered briefly, rallied into good humour – I remember being smiled at – and decided that we should be put on probation for six months, sentence suspended for two years, on condition that the parents made restitution to London Underground. This was estimated at twenty pounds each (Eddis excluded, naturally) which the father was able to pay from under the floorboard, and kept the change.

My father's references to the good opinions of me held by form- and housemasters weren't lies or fantasies, or even honest speculation, what he hoped they might have said if they hadn't known that we were up on criminal charges, because in fact they did know, headmaster, housemaster, formmaster – all of them

knew exactly what I'd done and had spoken of me exactly as my
father said they'd spoken, and this against the evidence not only of
the legal facts but their own experience of my moral nature – one
of my earliest reports had come right out with it and called me a
liar – well, not right out with it, it was one of those whimsical
schoolmaster phrases, 'sometimes a stranger to the truth', I think
it was – but that was straight out enough for the mother/Mummy.
'That a son of mine –!' the mother said, after waking me with a
slap in the face, then throwing the report at it – this was at about
seven in the morning, the report had arrived in the first post and
Mummy was in her transparent nightie but not her making-
breakfast dressing gown, 'that a son of mine,' she drew herself up
to her full height, thus revealing bits of herself that Hank Janson
wouldn't have wanted on his covers, 'should turn out to be a liar!'
'What about a son of Daddy's?' I might have asked, if I'd known
then what I know now – the scene ended with the father's voice,
calling from their bedroom in an unusually peremptory
fashion – 'Barbara – Barbara, can you come back in here, please!' –
perhaps he thought her reaction excessive, or had suddenly noticed
her dressing gown over the chair and realized that she wasn't
wearing it therefore, and the thought of her in my bedroom, as
good (?) as naked, slapping me about either alarmed the father in
him, or excited the husband. Anyway, she went to him with a
swivel of the heel, and I lay there, listening to their voices, his low
and even, hers tumultuous, dreading breakfast, which I knew
would be silent for me, noisy for Nigel – 'Are you playing rugger
this afternoon, Nige? Where will you be playing, darling – no, no,
I meant in what position, you fool!' with a cough of laughter and
a shower of ash, which I no doubt hoped would settle on Nige's
fried egg on toast. For me, of course, not a word, and only the sort
of looks that communicated that I was too revolting to be looked

at. That evening, when he took me through the report, the father concentrated on the academic rather than the moral side of things, worrying that I was bottom in Maths, and very nearly bottom in everything else except English and History. At the end he muttered, almost shyly, that by the way this business of my being 'a stranger to the truth' was a bit upsetting, wasn't it, old chap, perhaps in future I would avoid (he didn't actually say 'for her sake' but it hung there between us) telling even harmless little fibs, let alone large and necessary lies – if this is not the distinction as he actually made it, it's pretty well what he meant. Though what he really and most importantly meant was, would I kindly not get caught doing things that were reported in a report that would be read by my mother. That night, when I was back in bed, the mother made her goodnights by throwing open my door, stepping into the room to show me an icy profile with a cigarette in it, and then stepping out again, slamming the door behind her. I longed, naturally, for the usual cuffs and blows and laughter, longed for Mummy. My Mummy.

Got to stop for a while – it's a bit upsetting to find myself back there without being back there – they're both dead, the cunning child who loved and needed them has evolved or decayed into an elderly creature with a heartless memory – and did I love my father? I don't think –

LOVE, LAW AND ORDER

Distracted from distraction by an hour of television – an old *Law and Order*. Stroke of luck that it was on, and that I came in near the beginning. I love this series – love? Love *Law and Order?* – did I love my father? I don't think – Do I love *Law and Order?* – I know I do. Is it the word that's at fault, or is it my use of the word, or is it my self, my incapacity? Apply the Plato principle that we should love people for their virtues. What were my father's virtues? What are *Law and Order*'s virtues? – That's easy, just consider how it works: each episode has the same structure, three neat little acts. 1) The discovery of the crime (usually a body) and the police investigation. 2) The involvement of the DA's office and the arrest. 3) The trial and conviction – or sometimes the acquittal. Formally very dapper, you see, but flexible within its conventions – even though the official characters are always the same, and played by the same actors, there is a variety of story, of milieu, of incidental characters, played by those marvellous American character actors who give you a glimpse of a whole life in a two-minute scene – a grieving mother, an overworked guy behind a deli counter, a sixteen-year-old Hispanic with a gun under his bed and drugs in his pocket, so the scene-by-scene texture is terrific – as is the dialogue, snappy, authentic, moving the story along – and it's usually a pretty snappy and authentic story that's moved along, with often a twist that really twists – on top of which you get lots of detail about police work, along with lots of detail about the way the law works in New York – and in the one I've just watched, the conflict between the way it works in New York and the way it works, and doesn't work, in Los Angeles, made specially enjoyable by its exhilarating contempt for all things Californian – even to the faces, those round Californian faces, neatly featured, large shiny teeth, smoothly tailored hair, and there among them the New York faces, faces to which I am now addicted, slightly unhygienic, with pocks and other blemishes, slightly more used up, slightly more comically rancorous than the last time I saw them – So there it is, that's what I love about *Law and Order*. As for my father, Daddy, I –

we were swimming one summer afternoon on Hayling Island, probably the summer that Nigel and I came back from Montreal. The four of us were in the water, all four of us very good swimmers. The sea was calm, light waves, and we moved about in it in a little family pack until I found myself swimming away, heading out to sea as fast as I could until I was out of my depth, and then swam a bit further, and a bit further, the sea got colder, my body weaker, until I couldn't swim any more, the waves seemed to be rolling inside my head, I started to shake, pawing feebly at the water as I slipped under it, and the next thing I was in his arms. He'd kept an eye on me when I'd struck out, noticed the growing feebleness of my stroke, swum after me, gathered me in, carried me to shore. He laid me on a towel, Mummy poured tea from the thermos down my throat – 'Make sure it's got a lot of sugar in it,' he said. 'But what happened?' 'Nothing. He got a little cold, and outswam his strength, didn't you, old chap.' What has remained with me all my life was the feeling I had when I lay in his arms, my head against his chest, I was his child.

ON BEING A GENIUS

So. So. Well, back to the report. Whichever master wrote it would probably have been astonished by the emotional repercussions in 47 Oakley Gardens, he'd obviously used the phrase he'd used because he really didn't mind too much that I told lies, got caught out in telling lies, and in much the same spirit, I suppose, he didn't mind a couple of years later when I was caught thieving from the Underground – although he might have minded more if he'd known about my thefts at school, at the end of term, when I (and Quass and Eddis) would raid the lockers in our common room, extract the Latin primers, Maths textbooks, etc. and sell them in the second-hand shop located in the basement of Foyles – a practice we stopped when we started on the Underground, plenitude making us fastidious. Westminster was morally a wonderfully relaxed school – Quass, Eddis and I would surely have been expelled from any other public school in the country, but we weren't punished except that – well –

Our housemaster, Stephen Lushington, called me into his study and, in the most charming and graceful manner, put it to me that I should do my best to separate myself from Quass (the role of Eddis as partner in crime was unknown to him) as we were clearly bad for each other, and it was evident to him that I was the dominant influence – the Quass parents had said much the same thing to my parents, by the way – which is why he was addressing me on the matter rather than Quass – and perhaps I owed it to Quass, my friendship with Quass, to take the initiative in having less to do with him –

So when he came up to me to ask me, all – as I saw it – winks and leers and smirks, how the talk had gone, what had he said, in other words to share the joke of it, I did a little sidestep away from him, saying, 'Nothing, he didn't say anything really, excuse me, Quass, I've got to go home now.' So I cut him and snubbed him, and mostly felt good about it, even when I saw – as only I, apart from his parents, could – the hurt in the grin, the pain in the gloat. I felt I was cleansing myself of him and everything associated with him in my past, I felt that I was favoured by the authorities, was a special boy to them, to be watched and encouraged and even cherished, and that my disreputable past gave me an aura, a moral charm – yes, though I was known to be a delinquent, the specific nature of the delinquency wasn't known to anybody but the housemaster and the headmaster, as far as I knew, but it was generally understood to be a clean, clear, healthy, unsexual and uncorrupt delinquency, a sort of innocent naughtiness of behaviour that had landed me in a scrape somehow, briefly – and now here I was, a literary figure, winning school prizes for my essays, starting up a house literary magazine, there was a graceful swagger to everything I did, it seemed to me, no, that's not true, it seemed to me that it seemed to everybody else that there was a graceful swagger to everything I did, but really I lived in a chaos, an unchanging chaos, of desires.

And such was still my condition at seventeen and a bit when Daddy made his bacon-saving move to Halifax, Nova Scotia.

Bacon-saving for me, too. For one thing, it meant that I wouldn't have to do national service, for which, with my poet's sensibility and my masturbatory habits, I knew I was temperamentally ill-equipped – I'd got out of school corps after my conversion to the intellectual life by claiming that I was a conscientious objector, which was certainly true as I had the strongest possible moral objection to being ordered around by people I'd decided were inferior to me on the grounds that they weren't me, really, and therefore had no idea what was good for me and were thus post facto, ad hoc, de jure and any other Latin phrase you can think of, inferior to me, QED. Because I actually at the time did feel myself to be a most extraordinary and exceptional creature, a miracle of intelligent life, perhaps the only boy ever who'd travelled from Transitus C to Four B to Five A to the History Sixth (a preserve of the brightest and the best, only about eight of us accommodated) without knowing a single thing outside of myself – it's not that I didn't know, let us say, the dates of the kings and queens of England, it's that I didn't know that Charles I came before Charles II – it's true that given a little thought (but where was that to come from?) I could have worked it out, as I did know that one generally preceded two – really, it was more that my mind and body were hyperactively committed to their own needs, which took the form of self-celebration, self-worship. Well, look, every Friday I went to the cinema on the corner of the King's Road and – and – I can't remember what the other road it's on the corner of is called, but it leads down to Chelsea Bridge, and the cinema was called, I've got it! The Essoldo, yes – every Sunday, from when I became sixteen to the last Sunday before we enshipped to Halifax, Nova Scotia, I went to the first evening showing of the Special Sunday double bill, two old films, and both of them 'B' movies, in the hope that some scene would pop up in which there would be a girl bound and gagged, failing that, bound, failing that, with her skirt hitched to reveal a suspender and a stocking top, failing that, a stocking top. Once the film got going I would fall into the story, captivated even without a captive blonde, but what drove me to the cinema in the first place, whatever the weather, was the primary urge – and when I came out of the Essoldo onto the pavement, exhausted and exhilarated by either hope fulfilled (how could it be fulfilled? In public I was shy even of my own pockets) or hope denied – I say exhausted and exhilarated deliberately, because it was a combination of both, an almost mystical state that came from my reflection, this reflection, that I was by far the most intelligent person to have been in the cinema, by far the most intelligent, by far! I was a genius, I could tell I was, by my searing, scornful searchings of the other faces. I always hurried out, to be among the first through the doors, then cross the road to stand opposite the doors so I could see the other members of the audience leaving – so this was a deliberate and habitual event, every Sunday, this clocking of my inferiors, counting them off – more intelligent, better educated, than him or her or him – inspired, a poet, a genius, a very, very great genius, so established by mine own eyes, those comparing scrutineers as I stood on the pavement opposite the Essoldo Cinema on a Sunday night fifty years ago –

Things look bad for tomorrow, according to a television weather-woman – rather pleasant-looking and young – say forty-eight, or so – but with a nasal and downward-sloping voice – when I first came across that sort of voice I assumed that compassion-politics were at work, high-profile jobs for the vocally challenged sort of thing, but I've since been told that they're trained to speak like that, the idea being that they should sound not just not posh, but positively anti-posh – posh-bashing, I suppose it could be called – so what I was hearing from this pleasant-looking young woman of forty-eight or so was a posh-bashing weather report, promising rain tomorrow. Time to count my blessings, not out loud, though, nor on yellow paper.

PIERS, EARLY AND LATE

I was half his very big brother, who threw him up in the air, caught him, tickled him senseless, half his parent, who wheeled him about in his pram, toddled him to his nursery school, taught him to read and to swim. These were pleasures, although I pretended that I saw them as duties and that they weighed heavily on me. 'Oh, don't be so silly!' Mummy would say. 'You know you adore him.'

In his early drinking days, at Cambridge, he drank to be merry, sociable and free, he drank because he liked the taste, he drank because why not? – in Hong Kong he drank at first for the same reasons, and because that was what they all did in the Senior Common Room, but as the years went by and he went on delivering dazzling lectures on Wallace Stevens, William Carlos Williams, T.S. Eliot, to students who only wanted to master English as a commercial language, and writing long-pondered essays that though they were published were hardly noticed, and plays that didn't achieve productions outside Hong Kong (except once, at the Edinburgh Festival, posthumously) and finally a novel that was rejected with such brutality by a publishing friend that he couldn't bring himself to submit it anywhere else – through all this he drank more and more, from frustration and anger and then despair, more and more, eventually scheduling his day around his bottle. He became claustrophobic, so frightened in lifts that he had to walk up and down the many flights between his office and the common room, and of course, as he could no longer get on an aeroplane, had to give up his cherished vacations in London – in the vacations he kept to pretty much the same routine as in term time, but with the students and teaching omitted, and so with more hours to drink in. Every fresh term time his condition was worse, until finally he was incapable of teaching, became a nuisance in the common room, was banned from the campus, invalided out. He settled down in a flat a short walk from here, spending the hours he used to spend at the university in the Groucho Club, or visiting his old Cambridge friends – those with small children became less welcoming as they became more aware of the dangers – for instance he would suddenly lose control of his balance and topple abruptly to the floor, never actually on top of a child but sometimes close – he also began to lose control of his conversation, joining the same sentences together in an endless circle, and his mouth would suddenly fill with blood, one could see it before he gagged it down or lurched out of the room to throw it up in the lavatory. In his last weeks he would come around and sit silently in a chair in my study, his drink in his hand, his bottle of bourbon at his feet. His stomach was swollen, as were his ankles, which were visible between the turn-ups of his trousers and the espadrilles he wore without socks, even in the coldest weather, even in the rain. His face, though, was unlined, his blue eyes clear and alert – it was a beautiful face, that I had used to gaze at in wonder and joy when it was a baby's, and would now glance at surreptitiously, nearly fifty years on – occasionally he would catch my glance, smile with a serenity that seemed to have a taunt in it, raise his glass to his mouth – and I would turn back to my typewriter, clackety-clackety. From time to time I'd get him into a clinic, but he saw these stays, which he invariably cut short, as courtesies to me, and easily found secret routes to the nearest pub and off-licence – he treated doctors, counsellors, psychiatrists as opponents in a game, to be outwitted, every drink another point on his score card. When he was in his last clinic some friends came in a group to tell him that they could no longer bear witness to his self-destruction, if he didn't stop drinking, at least for a while, they would close their doors to him. He replied that he was sorry, but he couldn't contemplate life without alcohol. There was a long silence, and then one of them said, 'Well, Piers, you've just announced the end of our friendship.' And they left. A few weeks later he collapsed with a burst liver, burst kidneys, burst everything, really. His death caught him by surprise, I think – I certainly don't think he intended it, even though he did it by his own hand – but perhaps he had no choice, who knows? He certainly behaved as if he thought he hadn't, and all in all I'm pretty sure he wanted to go on living, if only to go on drinking. Every month or so I go up to Kensal Green cemetery and sit on the bench that Nigel and I had placed opposite his grave – a pretty spot, and the people who visit his neighbours are always friendly.

FEEDING THE ROT

I've just raked my pen across my yellow page, and jabbed it down and down and ripped it across. An attempt to write a primal scream. After all, I'm a writer and should be able to express everything, but here, once again, I've failed – who, on looking at these marks, would think they represented a primal scream without my having to say so – the need to do something savage was because I'd been sitting with my head in my hands, running my fingers through my hair and thinking how I really couldn't put down another word, I really couldn't, when it came to me that I wasn't running my fingers through my hair any longer because my hair had turned into maggots, long thin wiry and soft, climbing over and through my fingers, and then I realized that the bees were back, settled again into hollows in my body, the gigantic queen bee and her bustling mounds of worker bees, one set in each hollow of my body – kneecaps, elbows, and behind my forehead – behind my eyes – these hallucinations, if that's what they are, come to me when I'm depressed – a good thing too, one might say, otherwise how would one know one was depressed? Actually, that can't be strictly accurate, I used to have them a long time ago, before a continuous flow of hallucinations set in to do with vegetation and the colour green, that I was sprouting bushes out of my face, etc. – a phenomenon that I thought initially was caused by my alcoholism, then decided wasn't because they stopped coming long before I stopped drinking – but as I say, before that there'd been the bees and the maggots – no, not maggots first, worms first, so bees and worms before vegetation, and now, after quite a few years, bees and maggots – the difference between worms and maggots is not a pedantic one, the worms were fat and brown, the maggots, as well as being soft, are wiry and bright grey – it doesn't last long, this sensation of being a host to bees and maggots, and sometimes I can break the spell almost immediately, with a sudden vicious act – banging the table often works, or, as just now, with the written-down primal scream. I loathe the thought, though, that vegetation might follow, because the vegetation attacks were almost impossible to stop, I simply had to wait until they'd worn themselves out – some of them went on for a long time – I'm looking down at my hand moving across the lined yellow page – 'this warm hand, my scribe' – I don't know what to make of it, actually, I've had it all my life, I couldn't be more familiar with it, know it like the back of my hand, etc., but it suddenly doesn't look like mine at all, with its liver spots, wrinkles over the knuckles, a getting-on-in-life, down-at-heel sort of hand, go to bed.

I did. It's what I tend to do nowadays when confronted by a problem – mortality, for instance. In the old days I'd have taken a drink, and then another drink, possibly eight or ten drinks in a row, enough anyway to take me to a state that resembled tranquillity, but was really passivity – inertia, actually. Going to bed doesn't render me inert, although if I'm lucky I fall asleep. But before I fall asleep I lie on my side, with my knees drawn up as close to my chin as stiff joints, weak muscles and a pendulous stomach permit, the classic foetal position as adopted by a man sixty-five years away from the womb.

Ian's theory was these hallucinatory growths were healthy shoots of self-disgust, bursting out of my sense of my own moral rot, which is why, he said, they so revolted and frightened me. Otherwise, although they were initially alarming, why should I not come to accept them, welcome them even, as exuberant expressions of life and energy, springtime in the soul erupting through my body? This theory struck me as plausible because I did, in fact, feel at that time I was morally a shit-heap. My adultery, probably like so many other men's – I can't speak for women, I only know their side from books and films, not from conversations with women – odd, I almost wrote 'other women' – what would it mean, if I had? What does it mean, that I nearly did – actually, I can't speak for myself either, at least at this moment. 'The French do it better,' Ian would say to me, or I to him, 'That's only because they're French.' 'That's right. If we were French we'd do it just as well as they do it.' 'Absolutely. And if they were English they wouldn't do it half as well as we do it.'

MATTERS OF LIFE AND DEATH

Victoria has just come into the room, accompanied by George. George went to the French windows, out onto the balcony, and began the slightly mystical sniffing and peering through the railings that she does when she thinks, or so we think, that the fox is somewhere about, down in the garden. We talked about this rather as parents might about a daughter with a suspect boyfriend, imagining the possible conversations with George – 'Darling,' one of us might say, 'we don't want to be interfering, or snoopy, you know us, we respect your right to choose your friends, and I don't think anyone could call us – darling, what would be the word?'

'Specist?'

'Specious?'

'No, species. Spee-shees-ist.'

'Yes, nobody could call us spee-shees-ist, I hope, so it doesn't really matter that foxes are, as far as we understand it, rodents and not, like yourself –'

'Well, we don't know that, darling, do we, exactly, in what ways George is like or unlike –'

'Well, we know George sleeps on our bed, in it, sometimes, and sits on our laps. In our laps.'

'Well, we don't know that this chap wouldn't, given half a chance –'

'Yes, but apparently they don't house-train, nobody's ever been able to house-train them.'

'Them?'

'All I'm saying is that we don't know anything about him, George never invites him in. They hang about out there together, in the dark, doing God knows what –'

'Well, perhaps it's up to us to invite him in.'

'What! Like *Guess Who's Coming to Dinner* –'

'Well, why not, if he's anything like Sidney Poitier –'

'But that's just it, we wouldn't want him to be like Sidney Poitier, these days even Sidney Poitier doesn't want to be like Sidney Poitier.'

'Why do you assume he's a he, anyway? He could be a she.'

'Well, now you're opening a whole new can of – of –'

'Where's George?'

'She's there. Out on the porch.'

'No, she isn't. And there goes the cat flap, she's in the garden.'

'Unless George's invited him or her in.'

'Christ, if it knows how to work the cat flap –'

'It'll be in and out all the time. What about Tom and Errol?'

'They say they kill cats, bite off their heads and rip open their stomachs –'

'You know, I heard somewhere that the vermin people – you call them rodents, you see, you say you have a rodent problem, as if you're talking about rats, but it's understood that really you mean – you mean –'

'George's friend.'

'Well, let's get her in now. In and safe. You go down to the garden – I'll call her from here – George – George darling, hey George –'

So there it is. As with children, so with animals – you can't be too careful – oh, yes you can, with children – Ben at eight years old, insisting that he was old enough to walk to school by himself, everybody else did, every other boy and girl, he was the only one, the only one whose father clumped along beside him, he hated it, it made him feel he was just a baby, or that there was something wrong with him – well, I couldn't say that as far as I was concerned he was the only child in the school who was my son, and therefore the only one I wouldn't trust to cross the road sensibly, and as the road in question was the Archway Road, one of the busiest as well as one of the vilest in London, with lorries and those things that are three times, four times as long as lorries – pantechnicons, that's it. So up and down the Archway Road roar the lorries and the pantechnicons, with motorbikes careering on either side of them, it requires nerves of steel to cross the Archway Road with a child at your side, and inordinate patience to wait for the traffic lights to change, and though Ben had nerves of steel when it came to his own safety, he had no patience – so little that there were times that he tugged my hand so abruptly and powerfully that I thought he'd pull us both under the traffic – the short of it is that I refused for as long as possible, offering as a compromise that I would no longer hold his hand (though in fact keeping my hand close to the seat of his trousers), and that we would cross as separate individuals, as far as the world could see, not even related. I got away with two weeks or so of this, but of course he knew the other children knew, he could see that they were looking, laughing, jeering at Ben and his daddy, Ben's daddy and Ben, crossing the Archway Road together not, it was true, hand in hand, but hand by bum, and it was no good my saying that they weren't laughing and jeering (though they weren't, at least as far as I could tell), his view of his humiliation became so ferocious, his spirit and sense of honour, and no doubt his maleness, so diminished – all the girls crossing on their own, Dad, all the little girls, Dad – that eventually after long into the night agonizings we at last agreed to let him go to school by himself. It's actually very easy to follow a child, I discovered, children scarcely ever look around – at least they didn't in those days, comparatively innocent days. Nowadays, of course, children who are allowed to walk alone are probably trained to glance over their shoulders at regular intervals, and if they spot a man of the age I was then, in my late thirties, or indeed a man of any age, ducking and dodging along behind them, would know exactly what to do – and it's perfectly possible that even back then the parents taking the younger children to school would eventually have noticed me, and if they didn't recognize me as Ben's father, or perhaps even if they did, would have reported me to the police – but I had to stop doing it not long after I'd started because one morning Ben did behave exactly as I'd predicted, possibly because I'd predicted it – stood for a few seconds on the pavement, jouncing with impatience as he waited for the lights to change, then before they'd changed, when he thought he'd detected a gap, an alluring gap, in the traffic, darted into the middle of the road. Whereupon I bellowed BEN! Whereupon he froze. Froze in the middle of the Archway Road, with pantechnicons, lorries, motorbikes, run-of-the-mill cars, roaring at him from both directions, there he stood frozen, then turned, stared at me, I stared back at him briefly, he was obliterated by traffic for a lifetime of a second and then he turned up, so to speak, on the pavement beside me. In front of me, to be exact. 'What, Dad?' 'What?' I said. I couldn't say you nearly got yourself killed, as it was clearly I that had nearly got him killed. 'You nearly

got me killed,' he said, 'shouting like that.' 'Yes, yes, sorry, sorry, I
wasn't thinking, just saw you there, shouted without thinking. I was
going to the bank, you see.' No doubt gesturing towards the bank
which wasn't open at that hour, in those days, and in those days no
cashpoints of course. 'But you didn't wait for the lights, did you?'
There followed a brief but unattractive scene, a 'no, you didn't' 'yes,
I did' sort of scene, during which I managed to conduct him across
the Archway Road without his noticing. I decided never to follow
him again, better to spend an hour or so every morning not
knowing whether he'd killed himself, than be the cause of his death.
There's much in this story, now that I've remembered it, that seems
like a foretelling, or would it be a leitmotif, viewed backwards –
that my conscious efforts to help him always contain the elements
of his potential destruction – but on top of all this, this was my
point – I think it was my point – that the deep and frantic and
paralysing worry for one's children extends to one's pets – no,
actually it was the other way around – I got to Ben in the Archway
Road thirty years ago, by way of George and the fox in the garden
just now, and there's not just George to worry about, there are the
cats, Errol and Tom, what about them? Every day they risk being
run over. Or stolen. Both are very lovely, in their different ways –
and they have bouts of ill-health, Errol is becoming so fat he'll soon
have to go on a diet, sad for me as well as for him, as I love him fat,
the way he rolls about on the floor, his dainty waddle – and then
at the end, if they survive accidents, illnesses, kidnapping, there's
first of all old age, and then that awful bit past old age, when one
still can't bring oneself to give them up – for instance, Jeffry, named
in honour of Christopher Smart's cat, the first cat of my first
marriage. Jeffry wasn't much to look at – although he ate well he
always seemed slightly undernourished, with bandy front legs and
a small, peaky face – he was black, with short hair, a few white

splodges indented on his shanks – he was charmingly affectionate, good, quiet company, but slightly withdrawn and autonomous, in the way that cats are always assumed to be, though in fact not many are, and with a clear sense of what was owing to him – we had a piano in the bedroom, over the keys of which Jeffry would walk every morning, backwards and forwards, seeming to step on the same keys and tinkling out the same notes, until finally forcing one of us to get up to give him his breakfast. He was expert at catching mice and fledglings, the corpses of which he would leave for us as little gifts and surprises, either in armchairs in the sitting room, or on the dining room table. It was hard, of course, not to be disgusted by these offerings, and not to find oneself wishing that Jeffry wasn't so completely a cat in that one respect, but of course something in one was also touched and even grateful. All in all, he brought harmony into the house, and it was therefore a terrible shock when one day he wasn't there. He started his disappearance by not being there on the piano in the morning, and went on to be absent from all his usual places, all over the house, for all that day, and all the next. We asked our neighbours, put up posters, cursed his kidnappers – there were no signs of his having been run over, somebody would have heard, have seen – no, he'd been stolen, no question of it, some swine of an old lady or a besotted child had snaffled him off the pavement, claiming to themselves that he'd looked lost, starved, in need of a home – and at that time there were reports in the newspapers that a gang of cat-stealers went around the city in a van, taking cats and using them in some foul way for profit. It took weeks and weeks for Beryl to reconcile herself to the loss, though of course she didn't really, would still suddenly drop her book or leave the table and go on a wretched prowl up and down the street, or at the back in Highgate woods, calling for Jeffry, Jeffry. One day, when we were coming back with the shopping, a woman who was passing stopped, as if from an afterthought, and said, 'Oh, are you by any chance the people who've lost a cat?' Yes, we said, we were, we were. 'Well,' she said, 'there's a woman up the road in 84, the top-floor flat, who's found a cat.' Around we went immediately to 84, where a very nice woman, and her very nice husband, both ex-teachers, elderly and retired, showed us into the room where Jeffry was now living, in a large, cushioned basket, with soft drapings hanging down the side, and with saucers of water, milk, fish and chicken around it. He greeted us with a pleasant enough purr, though he seemed half-drugged with sloth and luxury. According to the woman Jeffry had followed her into the house one afternoon, accompanied her up the stairs and into the flat and proceeded to make himself so at home that she and her husband – he confirmed it – assumed that he'd been left behind by people who had moved from the neighbourhood. They had, she said, mentioned him to people now and then – no, no, she hadn't seen the posters on the trees – no, no, he hadn't seen the posters on the trees either – but then his eyes – he tended to walk with his head down – and she stepped straight out of the front door into the car when she went out, and she went out very little these days, and so, no, they hadn't seen the posters, but had mentioned to people now and then – all this over a cup of tea, with polite merriment, but that evening I expect there was as much grief in the top flat of number 84 as there was joy in the top flat of number 70 – 'But why can't they get their own bloody cat?' I said to Beryl, who said judiciously, compassionately, something to the effect that they were quite elderly, weren't they, probably didn't think it fair on the cat to take it on and then die, but if a Jeffry just walked in, offering himself, like little what's her name in *Silas Marner* – naturally we kept a bit of an eye on Jeffry after that, although it was comforting that we'd know where to look the next time he absconded – but can you abscond, unless you take something with you, somebody else's money or wife, for instance – but Jeffry had taken our love, our certainty in him, our faith – and his coming back, no, his having to be fetched back, what did it mean, exactly? He never went to number 84 again, as far as we knew – I'd hate to think that he did, and was turned away – and he behaved just as he'd always behaved, straight back to the keyboard for breakfast, etc., but still, there it was, he'd left us for a large basket with drapes and saucers of delicacies, was it a warning shot across our bows, a lesson in the instabilities of life? It was a bit of a mystery, an unsettling mystery, but it became an unpondered one eventually, as the years went by, and life without Jeffry seemed an impossibility until suddenly it became impossible not to notice that he was going, and impossible to do anything about it. He was really very old, the vet said, who was himself very young and called Justin – he could hang on for another few months, but don't leave it too late. But we did, we left it far too late, and later than that, we simply could not bring ourselves to do what we knew should be done, not until he was a spiky black sack, seeming to grind and creak as he tottered along the kitchen table, sometimes slipping to his knees but purring, that was the most piteous part of him, he kept on purring as if purring were a complete form of life in itself. And he stank; the stink from him was appalling. I took him to the vet in a taxi. He lay with his shrunken head on my lap, alternating his purrs with little whimpers of apprehension. The surgery was just off the Holloway Road, then a Greek-Cypriot neighbourhood, and standing in front of its door, as if they'd been alerted and were waiting for me and my pathetic bundle, was a pack of old ladies, five or possibly six of them, dressed in black – they swarmed around me as I crossed the pavement, making mewlings of sympathy and distress at the first sight of Jeffry, which turned into screeches of outrage and what sounded like ancient curses when they realized his condition, clearly they believed I had neglected, abused and even tortured him, which of course I had, in a way. I sat in the waiting room with Jeffry purring on my lap, stroking him and keeping my eyes lowered – I remember a couple of dogs, a torpid Labrador and a terrier with its leg in a sling, and there was a parrot with a bandaged beak – but I couldn't look at their owners, for fear of angry and reproachful eyes, and didn't dare look towards the window, sure that the old ladies would be glaring in, miming vengeance – people came and went, animals came and went, I longed for a cigarette, Jeffry purred and purred in that low, passive, haunting way until finally it was my turn and Justin came to look at what was on my lap. I couldn't meet his eyes either, but I heard the little noise he made. I followed him into the operating room, where he put on rubber gloves and got a syringe out of a box. I put Jeffry on the table. He scarcely stirred, except to stretch out his chin, with its white patch, but he went on purring. Justin put the syringe in, the purring stopped, and I went back into the waiting room, paid at the desk, keeping my back to the window, then slipped outside. There was just one of the old ladies standing there, a sort of outpost, I suppose, but she didn't notice me, her attention fixed on two small girls coming along the pavement, holding a cage – I couldn't see what was in it, but I hoped it wasn't past its kill-by date.

A LAPSE OF CONCENTRATION

Madame Me's a weed in bloom/ Self goes dogging everywhere is not how it goes, but how it comes out when I think of eight years of dogged, day-by-day, dutiful, not to say onerous adultery that I felt OK about only when I was abroad. Not that I wasn't adulterous abroad, but I didn't mind so much. In fact, I didn't mind at all. I would arrive in New York, for instance, with my wife-to-be, with whom I'd spend the first week, and depart with my wife, with whom I'd spent the second, and during both weeks I would be completely at ease with myself. So he didn't travel, perhaps he had no passport, or was quite simply a stay-at-home, this other, troubled adulterous self. I used to enjoy little glimpses of him in my mind's eye, a doppelgänger, moping in my study, or hanging about in a no-man's-land between two homes which were separated from each other by most of central London. But once I was back, taxi-ing west to north or north to west, breeding maggots, bees and worms in my moral system, with Ovidian translations into shrub, oak or cabbage in the offing – as I write this I try to keep a little of my concentration on the television in the corner there. It is showing *Meet Me In St Louis*. We've just got to Judy Garland singing 'Have yourself a merry little Christmas', but it looks to me – it's very charming, it's always charming, though I haven't seen it for years, but it does, quite truly, look to me as if she's been synched, her lips are doing the movements but not quite matching her voice – yes, it's probably me, these old eyes not matching these old ears rather than her young voice not matching her young lips.

We're past Christmas, now, into spring, we've got over the might-they-move-to-New-York-oh-please-don't! hump, and the whole family is at the fair, all the ladies in white (perfect for a day out) the young men (what else can one call them? although when you look at them closely, some of them are not particularly young, and quite a few of them not at all manly) wearing or holding those hats, the same shape as boaters but not made of straw – yes, there they are now, this marvellous family who've been living the same enchanting life for what, sixty years now, as freshly as ever, not in any way seeming to repeat themselves – that's the great thing about film, if you do it fresh in the first place it remains fresh for ever, on the stage you can be stale by the second night, though you can sometimes freshen up for the last night, it's true . As I write this, the eye aimed at the screen notices for the first time that one of the sisters, the oldest, looks much older than the last time I saw the film, perhaps she was always a bit elderly for the part and I've only just spotted it – I hope so, I'd hate to think that she's ageing away on her own, and that one day I'll find her on the screen looking like her Grandpa's wife – but isn't the Grandpa a marvel of acting, such charm, and effortless, I know him so well from so many films, but I've forgotten his name – I'll catch it on the credits, write it on the top of this page, ah, here it comes, the lights in the great state building are coming on, they stand together in the dusk, close together, admiring their city, their state, their country, happy, happy family, now the theme is swelling, 'Meet me in St Louis, Louis,' lightly it swells, and – fuck, it's over, gone from the screen just like that, the buggers, the shits, they've cut the credits, cut the credits, and something that looks like a roll of lavatory paper is unscrolling on the screen, and a voice too stupid for one to register whether it's American or English, or even what sex it is, is informing us of the programmes ahead, and so, along with the feeling that I've just been party to a brutal amputation, I realize I won't be able to write Grandpa's name on the top of the page. What I'll write instead is the name of the channel responsible, it's Hallmark, the Greeting Cards mob. Here you are, Hallmark. Here's a greeting for you. Two fingers in a V. And the same for my memories of adultery, come to that. Sufficient unto the day. And unto yesterday too.

3

STRANGERS ON TRAINS

– as I've got older I've developed a claustrophobia, a form of claustrophobia, in cars, more to do with the cars coming towards us or going past us than with the car I'm actually in – perfectly sensible, really, to be frightened in such circumstances, all you have to do is to imagine the guy high up in the pantechnicon that's running nose to nose with you, the big, boozed-up, unshaven, negligent-looking guy, one hand holding a bottle of beer and a bit of the steering wheel, the other hanging out of the window, a cigarette between two fingers jutted upright, and you just know that the eyes in the red pudding of a face are half-shut, the big belly full of turbulence and an ulcer, between the buttocks an abundance of swollen veins that cause constant heavy but sensitive shifts of balance, the whole body, in fact, a mass of disturbances, irritations, congestions, not to speak of a head full of dreams of a lustful and vengeful kind, and who's that old shit staring up at me from the passenger seat in that little what's-it, woman driver, yeah, move over old shit, tell your frosty little wife to move over, come on, nudge nudge, nudge nudge – what you say, a dawg and a cuppler cats? Well, who the fuck gives a fuck, gulp gulp puff puff puff nudge nudge old shit frosty wife two dogs and the fucking cat down the toilet – oh my arse these fuckin piles my ulcer gulp puff shit – is what I imagine going on up there in the cabin of the pantechnicon – which is why I travel by train, First Class smoker on East Anglia Railways.

This afternoon I had a table for four all to myself, on the table a couple of diet cokes, coffee very strong from the espresso bar at Liverpool Street, and Orwell's essay on Billy Bunter versus Miss Blandish for when I wasn't peering out of the grimy window, through the heavy drizzle, at a world that seemed to be all oblongs and squares, it was hard to tell whether streets or fields, town or country – it was all perfect, really, thinking of Victoria, Supervic, my wife, driving along, keeping cheerful company with George, Errol and Tom, listening to an opera on tape or the radio – the only irritation the usual businessmen on their mobile phones, but at least they kept their voices down, not much above the hum of the train, really, until three of them started up a rather loud conversation with each other – it had to be loud as they weren't sitting together, one was at the table for four up from me, the other two at small tables down from him, all of them with their backs to me, which was irritating as once they'd started I wanted to see their faces – it was one of those 'where were you when you heard it?' conversations – one of them had heard it when he was flying to Brussels, he was the nearest of the small-table men, the other small-table man had heard it at the end of a long lunch in Sheffield, while the third man, the four-table man, had heard it pretty well where he was now, only going in the opposite direction, a colleague had phoned him on his mobile at a few minutes after 3 p.m. – so that's when the back of the neck felt a little shiver, because I'd heard the news at the same time on what must have been the same train, in fact we were probably sitting in roughly the same relationship to each other then as now, and we must have been on our mobiles almost simultaneously, in my case I was talking to Victoria – she was driving back to London, with Errol, Tom and George, and I got her just after she'd made a detour to a small kennels from which she'd collected a puppy, a birthday present for my two granddaughters – hi, I'd said, I'm on the train, it left on time, everything was OK apart from the three or four businessmen all of them on their bloody mobiles, all of which had gone off within seconds of each other, bloody mobiles, I said down my mobile, how was she getting on herself, had she got the puppy? 'Listen,' she said, 'I think I've just heard something extraordinary on the radio, well, appalling if I understood it properly –' and she told me what she thought she'd heard if she'd understood it properly, and around me the businessmen were making noises that were probably identical to the noises I was making – and then we were at Liverpool Street, not empty exactly, but spectral, with a long, silent queue for the *Standard,* and its enormous headline, as if the enormity of the print would make the impossible credible. Then the tube, Holland Park and home. In my study, in the empty house, I sat slouched in an armchair and watched thinking that millions were watching with me, including, presumably, the clutch of men who'd organized it – sitting in a faraway cave, enjoying the replays, like a football manager and a spectacular goal – 'The lad did great.' Lads, in this case. The lads did great, dead themselves, six thousand dead others – or so the news reported – to prove how great they did. Victoria, George, Errol and Tom arrived at last. Victoria came straight to the television set. The others dispersed into the garden, eager to relieve themselves after a longish journey, part of which they'd shared with an unfamiliar puppy. Victoria and I sat in front of the television –

Now, on this train, probably the very same train but going the other way, I listened out for what the other chap had done when he'd got off at Liverpool Street, had he gone home to his wife, detoured to his mistress, dropped in on a pub with a television –

I felt an odd kinship with him – but he carried the conversation off in a different direction, to do with the effect on the market, share price index or whatever, one of the other men got up to join him, the third man began making phone calls, then sat down with the other two. When I got off at Stowmarket all three were at the same table but on their mobiles – perhaps to each other, a conference call to show they meant business – I wondered which of them was my one, so to speak – I fancied the one with the cigar. Actually, I'm not sure cigars are allowed, even in the smoking section, but I decided to let it go.

I had a twenty-minute wait at Stowmarket. It had stopped raining, but the platform was wet, glimmering in the late sun. I stood on it smoking and blank, happy I think, until there was the little train, more tram than train, on time to the minute, and almost empty. Again I had a table for four to myself, with a discarded *East Anglian Daily News* on the seat opposite, which contained news of local violence, quite a lot of it, really – rapes, burglaries, man shot in a garage, suspected irony in Ipswich – arsony, suspected arsony in Ipswich – no, arson, I mean arson, of course, in Ipswich, and outside Rougham a hit-and-run etc., all quite disturbing, but not quite as disturbing as the chap who suddenly sat down opposite me – I mean where had he come from, we'd left Stowmarket, we were on the move, he hadn't been standing or sitting nearby when I sat down, and furthermore there were lots of empty tables, even tables for four, for him to sit at, why did he want to sit with me, especially when he looked like what he looked like – he was about thirty years younger than me, and big, wearing a raincoat buttoned up to his chin, which meant, really, that when you glanced at him he seemed to be all face, and it was quite 'ugly' as we used to say in the olden days – disabled, do we say now, he had a disabled face? – button nose, small, stumpy teeth, and pop-out blue eyes which were popping out at me, and there was a sort of grin going on, well, anyway, a show of those teeth – his hands were under the table, I could sense them moving about, doing what? I remembered that murder some years ago on the London tube – the middle-aged man knifed to death by a young man who didn't like his smile, it was provoking him, he'd said at the trial (at which he was acquitted), it was personal. I tried not to seem personal, tried not to smile provocatively, and tried to concentrate on the paper, rustling the pages about and folding them emphatically this way and that and occasionally glancing at him casually, noticing his hat, a patch of mackintosh that slid over one ear, with a bit of a bandage sticking out from under it. So some sort of medical hat then, to protect an ear damaged God knows how, perhaps somebody had tried to bite it off – his girlfriend, perhaps, or his father – the eighteen minutes from Stowmarket to Bury seemed to take for ever and ever, I was convinced that he was going to reach under the table and grab me, I decided to get up, stuffing my stuff into my brown bag, but before I moved away, he stood and said something, which I didn't understand, except that want came into it, he wanted something.

'I'm sorry,' I said. 'What?' I waited for him to say my wallet, or my watch, or my brown leather bag, old and battered, or my life, in much the same state, but which I wouldn't give up without a squawk, though I'd virtually done my squawk with my 'what?' We stood with the table between us, staring at each other. Actually, I couldn't move – this was the moment foretold, kind of thing.

He spoke some more sentences, Suffolky sentences, which I completely understood. His newspaper. He'd left it on the seat to mark his place while he went to the toilet. His voice shook and I suddenly realized it was because he was nervous, possibly his eyes were popping for the same reason. It was costing him something, to speak up for what was his.

'Oh, oh I'm so sorry, I thought it was abandoned –' I took it out of my bag and handed it to him. It was a terrible mess, almost in a ball. 'Sorry. I didn't know there was a toilet on these little trains.'

He looked at the paper, made a stab at straightening it and folding it. He had small hands, clean, with neat fingernails. The toilet was down at the end, he said. By the last doors.

'Good to know,' I said. 'In fact, I think I'll –' and went there. I had a pee, did some work on my hair with my comb, and came out again, thinking to move to a different spot, but then remembered my bag and diet coke. I went back to the table.

It was the wife, he said. She expected him to bring it home with him in the evening. Otherwise it wouldn't matter. I had a sudden image of the wife, his ear between her teeth, he shaking his head about, explaining that this man from London had stolen it while he was in the toilet –

He seemed quite keen to continue the conversation, I could see now he was friendly, and potentially even garrulous, but we were coming into Bury and I could get away.

When I got off I looked back, from a sudden sense that there was something I hadn't done, or had forgotten. He was standing at the window, holding out my diet coke and plastic cup. I made a gesture that meant – or I meant to mean – too late, I don't want it, you have it. He smiled and nodded and the little train trundled off – I don't expect he'll drink the diet coke, or want to use my plastic cup, but I think things are OK between us now, which is what matters.

Victoria was waiting for me outside the station. We usually coincide there almost to the minute – while my train is being held up by a person being on the line or whatever, she is being held up by a pile-up on the motorway or whatever – and yet it's somehow always a surprise to see her, George in the front, on her lap, Tom and Errol in their baskets at the back, Tom crying indignantly. Errol, ever the master of his fate, comfortably dozing. It began to rain just after we left the station, and was raining more heavily when we got to the cottage twenty minutes later. As soon as we'd unloaded the car, I came across the garden to my study, and checked it out. The view from my London study is of a small garden, and then the backs of houses. The view from this one is of a small patch of garden, then a fence, and then a field that stretches and stretches – at night, if the moon is up, it is like the sea when it is completely calm. It is so tonight.

HEALTHY APPETITES

Just up the road there are the ruins of a manor house, with a moat and four swans, a mother and father who are a deep black, and two children, who are turning that way but haven't quite got there yet. They're nearly as big as their parents, but still have specks and streaks of grey, the colour they were when cygnets. I suppose they're in late adolescence at the moment, they've got the coarse manners, the greed and the bogus swagger – even in the water it's a sort of swagger – of adolescents, but they still hang about close to the nest, or never more than a foot or two from one parent or another, when they're out and about – a situation which the parents clearly find objectionable, particularly when they're having bread thrown to them. Victoria and I go up every evening to feed them, in all but the very worst weather – we feel guilty when we don't go, so really we should just go up whatever the weather, being wet being better than feeling guilty when it comes to these swans, who honk with pleasure when we appear on the rim of their moat with our carrier bag of crusts, honk out thank-yous when we leave. But in the passage in between, this is what I was aiming to get to – the parent–child relationship – the passage between, the unedifying brawl between the parents and children over the bread, the parents barging the children out of the way, the children barging back – this graceful and extremely well fed, not to say pampered family behaving in a style that would be called dysfunctional by social workers – my heart is always entirely with the parents, of course, partly because they're so devoted to each other – this evening, for instance, the father arrived with the two louts pounding gracefully along behind him, began his butting and barging the moment I began to throw the bread (I do the feeding, Victoria stays a few feet behind with George. Victoria is convinced that George, unless kept closely restrained, would hurl herself into the moat in an attempt to snatch a crust from their beaks) but broke suddenly away, mid-gobble, and swam towards his wife, who'd just decided to climb down from the nest – as ungainly a sight as you'll ever come across, a swan manoeuvring its way down a river bank, its large body pitching and swaying, its paddle feet slipping and skidding under that lushly feathered bum, then the clumsy crash into the water – then lo! the smooth and haughty glide of her – and there was old dad, back turned on the kids and the goodies, gliding towards her, and when they were a few feet from each other they each made a small, loving honk, and dipped their heads at each other, then moved in together, butting and barging the kiddies off the goodies. They had all the zest this evening, of a strong and loving marriage, it made the heart soar, well, made us laugh with pleasure – my, how we did laugh, Victoria and I, as we moved on to the pigs with our carrier bag in which were apples and old lettuce leaves and cabbage stems, potatoes, etc. There are four pigs, to go nicely with the four swans, and their sty is set in a large patch of nettles and bushes, with some cleared terrain so that they can roam about, when not slumbering on top of each other in their sty. Like the swans they've learnt to identify our voices and tread – they have a rather terrifying way of not being there until there they are, surging out of their sty or one of the beds of nettles, groaning and snorting with desire, and although they're not a family – well, they may be related, a brother (a great sack of testicles and an enormous snout) and his three sisters, or perhaps they're cousins, I don't know, must check this out – they're not parents and children is what I mean – they behave as brutally with each other as the swans do, butting and barging, with the brute male of course winning out, or would do if we hadn't learnt to distract him by tossing the first fistful of fruit and veg straight at him, then moving a short distance along the fence and distributing to the other three, who at least fight it out on equal terms, until he's back amongst them, lettuce leaves hanging out of the sides of his mouth, his jaws grinding away at an apple, the juice of which spurts and dribbles and foams around his jaws, which he tries to jam into their share even when he's got no space available in his mouth to snuffle it into – and they of course banging and butting back at him as they gobble down whatever they can pick up. There is no enjoyment here, no pleasure in the appetite, no, it's anarchy, an anarchy of greed, gluttony as a state of war – and yet there is the alternative and incontrovertible fact, that when there is no food on offer they lumber about together in a small, cheerful sort of herd, and as I think I've already noted, sleep, or doze or just lie fully conscious in a pile or heap, on top of each other, higgledy-piggledy.

UNHEALTHY APPETITES

– sad, ironic, and animated may be synonyms but they don't get it, in fact I suspect the truth is that there's no such thing as a synonym, if a synonym will do instead of the word you're using then you're probably not using the right word, so let's leave it that his eyes were full of a wry, lively, melancholy – why am I picking over this so daintily when actually all I want to say is how sweet and loveable he was in his frailty at that time, facing first the prospect that the chemotherapy wouldn't work and the tumour remain inoperable, therefore facing the prospect of a slow and painful death, then the prospect, if the chemotherapy worked, of a long and complicated operation during or after which he might die, and then, at the very best, the prospect of a long and humbling convalescence, when for a time he would be far weaker coming back to health than he'd ever been when he was ill. That was the future he faced, and occasionally talked about. Talked also of course about many other things, seemingly unrelated but all of them somehow stemming from this central fact in his life, that his death was inside him, working busily a-day, busily a-night, busily striving to bring itself to a triumphant negation even as he sat talking about it – and then what does it do, does it move on, does a tumour move on? Is it a separate and individual life form, a sort of galactic immigrant that leaps from host to host – I was going to say indiscriminately, but perhaps not indiscriminately, perhaps discriminatingly, choosing according to its own needs and laws, and from an appetite for more than just survival – perhaps there's a variety of cancer that has an appetite for writers, attracted by their temperaments, then picking out playwrights for the fertile contradictions of their circumstances – that they work in solitude, then expose the work of their solitude in an indecently public, manner, etc., finally homing in on Harold as the perfect example of this playwriting species, and therefore a perfect host, given its own sophisticated and refined tastes –

– actually, the best account of Harold and his tumour is from Harold, in a poem which shows him in intimate, playful, almost doting contact with it – this poem, by the way, which Harold called 'My Cancer', this product of an intensely private communion with what was intent to kill him, was published in newspapers throughout the world, indeed on the front pages of some of them, which leads us to meditate briefly on the nature of fame – who would have heard of Harold's tumour if it hadn't chosen Harold? I must look up in the dictionary the connection between tumour and tumescent, by the way, if there is one. The latter can't be the adjective from the former, surely?

I've just written him a letter – Victoria drove me six miles to Bury, where I posted it so that it would get to him forthwith – well, not forthwith, given the current state of our postal service, perhaps within a week or so. Not that it contained anything particularly interesting, though it might cost him some much-needed strength to find that out, as he has difficulty reading my handwriting – everybody does. I do myself. In fact, I sometimes think that's how I got a decent degree – the examiners taking the easiest route when confronted with page after page of illegible script – just my name readable, and certain key words – 'dichotomy', 'paradoxically', 'Manichean', 'metamorphosis' and one or two suggestive ones – 'uxorious', 'muffins', etc. Nowadays, of course, when students have to be computer literate, which is just a high-tech way of saying they can't read or write – this is nonsense. Stop it.

QUESTIONS OF STYLE AND TASTE

Last night I began revising a paragraph because I was shocked by what I was writing even as I was writing it. So I softened it, sweetened it a little, softening and sweetening myself a little too in the process, and then I thought, but no, this is fraudulent, leave it as it was, so I went back to what it was, ran my eye through it, made a correction to one of the sentences because it looked gauche, and then I was at it, and by at it I mean working at it as if it were a piece of writing, I must have spent hours on a few paragraphs, fretting away at sentences, arrowing them in and out of each other, then doing a fair copy which I then rewrote, and again copied, and so on until the old headache began, the brain felt arid, the sentences on the page were as dead as counters – tiddlywinks, as if I'd been playing tiddlywinks for an eternity, but without a cup to wink the tiddle, tiddle the wink into – it wasn't until I was undressed and about to get into bed that I realized what I'd been up to, so I had to get dressed again, put on boots because it was now raining, clump across the garden, rip the pages out of the pad, tear them into strips, screw them up and bin them, then back across the garden, hating the dawn light, the birds, the rain. 'I thought you'd already come to bed,' Victoria mumbled. 'No. That wasn't me,' I said. 'Who was it then?' she said. 'Bob Monkhouse,' I said. It cheered me up, this exchange, it cheers me up to remember it now, as I put down this resolve, that I will never again rewrite any part of this, on I go and on – feckless, thoughtless, cruel and stupid, it doesn't matter, because in this case you are only what you write, never what you rewrite – there's a football match, a pre-World Cup friendly between England and one of the Koreas. I have to watch it, for professional reasons.

Christ, we were dreadful, especially in the second half. Trevor

Sinclair seemed determined to get the ball to South Korean feet, which involved him in perverse displays of skill, as it would sometimes have been easier to get it to English feet – but that's not what really incensed me, what really incensed me was – is – that 'to be fair' has now become a sort of tic with sports commentators, every other sentence, sometimes two in a row, beginning with 'to be fair' – 'to be fair on the lad', which is how one of them began a sentence on Trevor Sinclair, 'to be fair on the lad, he did play very badly,' that's what he actually said. And then there's 'reinvent', you see it and hear it all the time, somebody has 'completely reinvented' herself as a feisty, foxy, tart or fart, whatever – now why do I find this so irritating, no, worse than that, offensive, and tinged with a kind of blasphemy – well, for one thing, in order to reinvent, you have to invent, and who therefore is this self-inventing and self-reinventing self, rather like that definition of God as thought thinking on itself, yes, that's it, I suppose, people who say they have reinvented themselves are thinking of themselves as god-like, and people who describe other people as reinventing themselves are attributing god-like powers to the self, which is a poor, miserable, partly suffocated thing, on the whole – I suppose that really all they mean, the hordes of journalists etc. who are so addicted to the phrase, is 'change', but that's a simple word that contains, when applied to people, some proper element of mystery – 'he changed. He became a good man.' And what about 'majority'? 'He played the majority of the game with a bad leg' – what's wrong with 'most' for most plurals, 'most of the people in the room', etc., saving 'majority' for when it's really useful, as in opposition to the minority, etc. This morning, in the *Independent* I think, though it may have been *The Times*, we were told that Roy Keane is 'flaunting the rules –'

Why do I care? Why does it make me so angry? Is it something that happens to you after a certain age? Ian and I used to paint the picture for ourselves, two old guys sitting in the corner of Chez Moi, full of rancorous pedantry, and of course it was fun when we were being rancorously pedantic together, making a game of it and ourselves into a joke, but I think we always minded, even when we were young, and then began to mind more when we suspected that almost nobody else did, much. Or noticed even.

On the other hand, I've recently heard myself using phrases quite alien to me – borrowed, really, or are they inherited? from my parents' generation. I used to hear them when I was growing up, a play 'was really rather amusing', they used to say and I now say – said just the other evening – and it was of a play that I'd actually disliked – we were at a party, friends of the playwright were present, and the odd thing is that I couldn't for the life of me have said anything good about the play, couldn't have brought myself to tell a clear, direct lie, but said easily, without any sense of a moral tremor, that I thought it was 'really rather amusing', which was accepted all around as a compliment, and I was happy to let pass as one. And at another point at the same party, I told someone I'd never met before that a mutual friend was 'absolutely delightful' – well, I mean she's lots of things, intelligent, obstinate, sometimes stupid, and sometimes sexy, etc. – an endless list of attributes I could have come up with, we could have discussed them and the contradictions implicit in the list, but no, I chose to say that she was 'absolutely delightful', and said it with a kind of drawl, like George Sanders, or BoBo's husband, Mr Carew, or even Mummy, come to that, she'd have said it with a drawl, too, and a flourish of her cigarette. So one comes at last into one's inheritance – as they spoke in their thirties, so I speak in my sixties.

And by the way, the words 'disgraceful' and 'disgusting' seem to

be perpetually on my lips these days – generally applied to some
news item about the National Health or education or the prison
system or almost any journalist – one columnist, for instance, is
'quite disgraceful', another 'absolutely disgusting', again Mummy's
formulations, with her intonation – though not her contexts,
which were more personal – her *bête noire*, the man in the little
chemist's shop in the King's Road, was 'absolutely disgusting', while
the behaviour of Jenkins, who owned the dairy on Chelsea Manor
Street and delivered our milk, was 'quite disgraceful' – I don't
remember what he did, or kept on doing.

A PRACTISING PLAYWRIGHT

What has happened? Do I remember what has happened? We left
Suffolk for London again. That's one thing that's happened. In
London I discovered I've got cancer. So that's another thing that's
happened. And now we're back in Suffolk again, so that is yet
another thing that's happened – ever since we got back here I've
been struggling with the play about the people on a Greek island –
I've been thinking of moving them to a remote part of Turkey, to
make them feel more anxious – me too, as I've never been to
Turkey – would I have to do research, even go to Turkey, some
remote part of it, so that I could write with authority – write what
with authority? Well, the stage directions, I suppose, 'The play is
set in a remote part of Turkey,' – write those exact words which I
have in fact already written at the top of the play (except I've
written Greece, not Turkey) – but with authority this time, because
I'd actually been there. Or I could invent some part of Turkey that
was so remote nobody would know whether it existed or not,
except me – like that friend of Dr Johnson, who claimed he'd been

to China and wrote an enormous book about it, describing the country – the landscapes, the people, their customs etc. – all of it completely made up and complete nonsense, but completely believed in by the London literati – I like to think that Dr Johnson himself had doubts, but that they didn't affect their friendship. Of course these days most people have been everywhere, including remote parts of Turkey, either by plane or by television, and the theatre reviewers amongst them would complain that either my local detail is inauthentic, or its absence suspicious, spending the rest of their reviews furnishing authentic local details of their own, under a headline in which the word turkey would figure in its several senses – 'A turkey from Turkey' for example. Better leave the play in Greece, I've been there quite often, after all, though mainly for the swimming – the most beautiful water I've ever been in is around the island of Spetses, though much of the local detail, authentic local detail – the restaurants with their unflushing lavatories located in the middle of the kitchens, the fingernails of the waiters, the condition of the plates and cutlery, not to mention the food itself – you wouldn't expect to see an authentic Greek restaurant on any but a subsidized stage, where they might do it in the style of those Neapolitan plays, but instead of the mouth-watering smells of Mamma's pasta sauces wafting out to the audience there would be the traditional Greek smells of bad fish being fried up in the oil they were using last year too. I still haven't done Mummy's football boots, while I'm on this sort of subject.

STILL NOT MUMMY'S FOOTBALL BOOTS

Antonia's edited a small selection of Harold's poems, twelve of them, and they all seem to me to be – well, poems. Real poems.

Which is one of the highest human achievements, in my view. Antonia has chosen with wifely insight – most of the poems are about her, quite rightly, as they are among the best along with the poems about death (one on the death of his old English teacher) and the one about cancer. It makes me wonder whether the rest of Harold's poems are better than I thought – probably not – after all, a dozen decent poems is as much as a man should expect to write in a lifetime, and as Harold's life is quite distinctly not yet over, there may be one – or even two – more. And Hardy wrote his greatest poems when he was about Harold's age. But Hardy had a spirit that nourished itself on pain, most of it inflicted by himself, much of it on himself. One wonders what he felt after he'd written 'After a Journey' – so much yearning, remorse, grief so powerfully and perfectly expressed might have left him with a feeling of placid triumph, yes, done it again, and a special thank-you to the dead wife for serving first as victim, then as subject, and what an alchemist I am, turning the dross of my behaviour into the gold of my verse, and talking of dross, what about that dress of hers, the blue – wasn't it? – dress, yes, there's a poem in that somewhere, do I see it, don't I, that dress? No, gown, gown, air-blue gown and off – 'Woman much missed, how you call to me, call to me . . .' – was his remorse intensified by expressing it, in fact added to by knowing he was going to enhance his reputation by publishing it – he was, after all, a professional. Sometimes, these days, when I've spent hours on the typewriter I feel that I'm a reverse alchemist, no, a negative reverse alchemist, in that I take the dross of my life, of my understanding of life, and turn it into something drossier. The fact that Hardy wrote some of his best stuff at the age that Harold's writing some of his best stuff, doesn't give me the right to think that at my age I can do anything at all except the physical business of battering the shit out of the typewriter, no, battering shit out of the typewriter, about people on a Greek island who can't even go to Turkey – really, I'm only sticking at it as a distraction from my cancer. A little cancer, apparently – like a little pregnant? No, this little cancer is a perfectly self-contained creature, nestled there in my prostate with no plans for growth, as yet anyway, or so say the two urologists I've spoken to. But of course the pattern is unmistakable – from Ian, to Harold, to me, Harold overlapping with Ian, I overlapping with Harold, like a poisoned baton in a relay race – though the simile doesn't work out as Ian is dead, Harold is recovering, and I am merely nursing a little cancer, giving it house room, really, as we did with the cat Errol, who began by straying (quite deliberately, a planned stray) into our kitchen one afternoon, then annexed room after room in the most affable, no, loving manner, and now sleeps on our bed with George, and rolls around the sitting room in George's arms, and otherwise just lounges around the house as if he's paid off the mortgage – but you can't really compare Errol to the little cancer in my prostate, if the cancer annexes organ after organ it won't be in an affable, no, loving manner, and rolling around in whose arms where etc.?

Naturally, I brought it all upon myself by contracting bronchitis when we were in Suffolk the last time – at least, I did if you look at it this way: my smoking brings on my bronchitis: my bronchitis brings on my doctor, who brings on a blood test: the blood test reveals that my PSA (prostate something and something else) is high, twice what it usually is, and it's usually more than twice what it ought to be anyway, which makes my current PSA more than four times what it ought to be; and so on to a physical examination, ultrasound, biopsy – biopsy, absolutely not, I said to my pleasant and intelligent if – in my view – hyperactive doctor, 'you know perfectly well that I don't do biopsies, most particularly in the prostate,' and he did know, having sent me on three previous occasions, from each of which I'd fled, expostulating that I couldn't, just couldn't and what's more wouldn't – I'd concede that it's an irrational response, a phobia, except that it seems to me a rational response, normal. Perhaps what it means is that I'm a rectal virgin, having gone through prep school and public school and all my adult life without having my rectum probed by anyone – and the thought of it, the mere thought of anything not attached to myself touching me there – but all this is no longer true. The truth is I am no longer virgin. I was ravished by a lady doctor who did what the Victorian ravisher did to the little girl in Larkin's 'The Less Deceived' – she doped me with a special, opium-free concoction, and when I passed out, had her way with me – though you wouldn't have thought so if you'd seen her immediately afterwards, her cute little face, mid-forties, I'd guess, possibly fifty, the age at which I now think women are growing towards their most very attractive – she looked neither ashamed nor sexually spent, just cute. She said how good I'd been, brave and obedient, while unconscious.

Victoria took me home in a hired car, and I ate yogurt and honey, and took George and Errol to bed with me, lay there for the rest of the afternoon, and then watched a Steven Seagal film. I am a Steven Seagal fan, loving his retro ponytail, his lushly muscled body with its hints of corpulence to come, his quick-footed, buttock-rolling walk, and above all the softly growling tone in which he issues warnings of death or castration. I would say that in his actions he's a man's man, a man's once-upon-a-time man, but in his style he's a touch womanly – the large, child-bearing hips, and the circle of fat around his stomach that suggest he's in touch with the chocolate and milkshake child within. In one of his films he plays an eco-warrior, shooting holes in different parts of Kris Kristofferson (also terrific) while explaining to him that he isn't going to kill him, he's going to turn him over to one of the prisons, where the convicts would do to him what the cute doctor had done to me, only with unsterilized instruments, I would imagine –

So my hyperactive doctor phoned on Friday afternoon and left a message on my answering machine – the biopsy results had come in, there was something in them that would require some serious discussion, looked forward to talking on Monday. Monday. Monday seemed a long way from Friday, with such a message on the mind. Saturday, Sunday and Monday came and went, Dr Hyperactive being hyperactive in other areas of interest. Most of Tuesday went before I made contact with Hyperactive's partner, who regretted that Hyperactive had been out and about for the past two days, but here, by chance he happened to have my prostate results before him, I had cancer, these were the possible treatments – 1) radiotherapy, his personal favourite for my case, which involved six weeks of daily visits to a hospital near you, only drawback being that it would cause some – perhaps more than some – fatigue, and could bugger up the stomach – in my case further bugger up the stomach; 2) an operation, out of the question in my case, given my allergy to anaesthetics; 3) hormone treatment, painless, easy, convenient, adieu to the sex life however; and 4) something to do with needles thrust up the anus into the prostate, where they would lodge for – I can't remember how long they would lodge for, months, years, until death. And that was it, those were the options, Hyperactive himself would be in tomorrow, to pick up the threads. The next day Hyperactive, full of apologies – 'I won't bore you with the details of my ghastly weekend' – took me through exactly the same list again, named the urologist to whom I was to go, fixed the appointment, and so – and so it's creeping towards five in the morning, the light is changing, birdsong on its way, I've taken a sleeping pill, and my head is full of shapeless stuff –

A SMOKING UROLOGIST

It's half past one in the afternoon, and on television England are playing a test match at Lord's. The sun is strong, this is an English summer's day of the childhood kind, butterflies are tumbling in and out of my study windows – actually a shed in the garden, have I mentioned this, but with mod cons, yes, I have mentioned it, but probably didn't mention that in one of the drawers of my desk I keep a hospital-type plastic bottle in which I pee when it's too cold to open the door. When it's warm I turn right on the step, unzip, hose down the flower bed, good for both of us, I like to think. A very large bee has just rollicked in, rollicked about, rollicked out, more Disney than Suffolk, really – my granddaughters Maddie and Gee-Gee are romping naked in a paddling pool so enormous that I feel it would kill me to do a couple of laps in it – they're naked, these plump and wholesome little girls, pink and white and stark naked, and if I wished I could stare smiling at them through the window – but then of course I imagine myself being observed by a passing social worker or policeman – smiling through the window at two naked little girls plunging about in the paddling pool, and then I imagine the police station, my face, cheeks swollen, small eyes squinting their guilt, etc., and so, reflecting sombrely that it's not only the children that have had their innocence stolen, it's grandpas too, better keep my head bent over my yellow pad and write down my thoughts on urologists – or rather the two urologists I had dealings with, one last week, one the week before. First first. His office was in Wimpole or Harley, one of those, several floors up, reached by a lift. We were greeted by his receptionist, an eager young woman who nevertheless had something troubled about her. She led us into a diminutive reception room, in which a sturdy black man in his early fifties, I'd guess, was sitting with his hands clamped on his knees, staring into a horrifying future. The receptionist, obviously acutely conscious of this chap and the state he was in, sat down at her computer and concentrated on it. Victoria and I went in for strained banter, trying not to look at the black man who almost filled the other side of the room – eventually the receptionist said, 'Here you are,' with a nervous, sideways look towards us, and handed him a sheet of paper. He looked at it with first suspicion, then outrage, 'I'm not paying this!' he shouted. 'I'm not paying, no, no, out of question, out of question!' He had a Spanish or a French accent – a bit of a surprise considering how English his togs, how sturdily English middle-class – old-fashioned middle class the effect of him when silent – 'I better had operation, operation cheaper than this.' 'Oh, but –' the receptionist said, and tried to explain that no, he was getting off comparatively lightly, the operation would have been much more expensive than the treatment he'd had –' (Actually, I might be getting it the wrong way around, he might have had the operation and now wished he'd had the treatment) and so it went on, except it got worse – at one point he flung the paper to the ground. He had a powerful voice, which got more powerful as the receptionist continued, carefully, gently, to defy him with mathematics, further bits of paper, etc., and he was, in fact, demanding to confront Mr X, the consultant himself, when the consultant himself, Mr X, in his pinstripe suit, his Barbados tan, and his deaf smile, entered the room, took the necessary three steps to place himself in front of us, and introduced himself, 'Do come into the office,' he said, 'Do come into the office,' and somehow managed to walk back around the black man, who'd stood up and was flourishing the bill at his averted cheek. We followed him into his office, which was so just around the corner from the waiting room that it might as well have been in it, and as we sat down the row started up again, somehow louder for being invisible. Mr X picked up a sheaf of papers, presumably my notes. He was an uninteresting-looking man, anonymous, a composite of everybody's idea of the professional man, but this may have been achieved by an act of will. He turned over the pages expressionlessly, then folded his arms across his chest, and asked us if we had anything to say. I said we were there to hear what he had to say. All he had to say, he said, half getting out of his chair, was that this wasn't a wait-and-see situation, action had to be taken as soon as I'd had a bone scan which would determine whether the cancer was spreading, all right? his receptionist could fix the appointment for the scan immediately, all right? Well, I said, or Victoria said, could we perhaps discuss how things would go if – no, he said, speaking through the din from around the corner, no point, wait for the results of the bone scan, all right? He touched the seat of the chair with his bum, then stood up, led us out into the hall, gesturing us towards the door as he then proceeded back into the waiting room. I caught a glimpse of him standing sort of side-on to the black man, asking him, in a politely surprised voice, if he wanted to see him, by any chance. Then we were in the lift, and away. I think the reason I never want to see Mr X again isn't that there was a row going on in his waiting room, nor that he'd rushed us through the session from embarrassment, nor that he'd either read my notes for the first time in front of me, or had pretended to – it was his tan that turned the knob on him, as far as I was concerned. His tan. His tan in pinstripes, so to speak. Why? I go to Barbados myself, come back much more tanned than he, and if I don't put on pinstripes when I settle to my work then that's a perk of my profession – consultants wear pinstripes, writers wear whatever they like, pinstripes included, come to that, or bunny clothes, or nothing –

so how could I blame him for his pinstripes or his tan, furthermore, he was probably far more entitled to a holiday in Barbados (why did I assume it was a Barbados tan, it might have come from India or Florida) than I, contributing vastly more to the well-being of society by looking after its prostates, than I with my plays, which might, for all I know, contribute to the ill-being of society, the cause of prostates which he in turn treated, thus earning the money that took him to Barbados, or India or Florida or all three annually – but to hell with all that, I wasn't going back to him, nor was Victoria – but then why should she, she doesn't even have a prostate, except by proxy – we'd find someone else.

So to the second urologist. I'd sat next to him at the fiftieth birthday dinner of the friend who recommended him, and inasmuch as I remembered him I remembered liking him because he smoked – a smoking urologist was bound to be my sort of urologist.

Actually, he wasn't my sort of urologist, when it came to it, as he a) was of the view that my liver and stomach were such a shambles that I couldn't expect to live long enough for my prostate to become a serious threat – especially given my smoking habit, b) had himself stopped smoking. What made his verdict on my life expectancy particularly hard to bear was that he repeated it a number of times, as if I were wilfully denying it, which I wasn't, and each time with an apology either at the beginning or the end – 'I'm sorry to have to say this but –' or – 'but there it is, sorry.' I liked one part of his news, though, the no point in treatment part of it – well, not the 'no point' part of it, the 'no treatment' part of it. And at least he didn't have a tan, in fact he had the opposite of a tan – big white face, big white teeth, not much hair, large white hands – and he wasn't anonymous – in fact he was the opposite of anonymous, bags and bags of personality, some of them recently added, I suspect, to compensate for not smoking – so all in all, if he wasn't strictly speaking my sort of urologist, he was the sort of urologist I ought to have. And so I have.

The next day brought the bill, for one hundred and thirty pounds, from urologist number one. We'd seen him for about seven minutes, a few of which he'd spent reading – or pretending to read – my notes, another two of which he'd spent mute, with his arms folded across his chest – so let us concede that these were both urological acts, and justly included in the bill, why then, he was valuing himself at fractionally under twenty pounds sterling a minute. I can't wait to see urologist number two's bill. He gave us more than twenty minutes of his time, all of them filled with speech, which would work out at – let's not work it out. The big question is whether I pay urologist number one's bill. I put it in one of those drawers, and we came down to Suffolk, and here I am now, sitting in my study – see me now, sitting in my study – see him now, sitting in his study, anticipating a smooth run to his eightieth birthday, when he will be found in his favourite armchair, slippered feet resting on his favourite cat, head bowed over his favourite poem, by Hardy, of course, his lips trembling out his of course favourite lines, 'He never expected much/ Just simple-minded slaps and such', and outside the grandchildren dumping in the paddling pool, the butterflies humping in the woodshed, the plumple bees drifting drowsily on little eddies of insecticide, a life spinelessly lived, now supinely closing –

Tomorrow is going to be another lovely day, a woman with a set smile has just said on television. She was talking of the weather. What I liked about her was that she didn't seem to care much, one way or the other.

DIFFERENT SPECIES

Last night, when I'd stopped poking uselessly away at the Greek play, I took a couple of Co-proxamol – a sort of aspirin for people whose stomachs can't take aspirin – and a sleeping pill. I then turned on the television, and looked for something that would soothe or excite thoughts of my life expectancy out of my mind. I came in in the middle of a film I've seen a few times before, *Species*, it's called, science-fiction horror about an alien who's taken up residence in the exceptionally beautiful body of a young American woman, with the express object of breeding with a human male, and so peopling (clearly not the right word) our little planet with her own kind – her own kind, when it emerges periodically from the body, or rather through it, is a more than routinely revolting piece of work – stolen, of course, from *Alien*, but with some thoughts added, for instance a tongue, softly and eagerly probing in a French kiss, suddenly transforms itself into a sort of slithering turd with ridges and spikes, that shoots straight through the aroused male's mouth and out of the back of his head – this occurs when the alien, inexperienced as yet in sexual practices, and unused to desire, loses herself to itself, so to speak, and so foils herself and itself of what it most needs – no, that's not quite it, itself needs procreation, herself needs sex. In the end they achieve both, and the expression of ecstasy on her face as it feels conception beginning as her orgasm ends! – this alien is a very rapid breeder, by the way, so rapid that twenty minutes later she's down in a sewer (in flight from her pursuers, among them Ben Kingsley – class, eh?) having contractions, and a few seconds later, there among the scampering rats, she delivers herself of a little flock of aliens, garbed as children, almost Pre-Raphaelite in the sickliness of their charm and innocence – until one of them flicks out its tongue and pulls a passing rat into its mouth – and it was exactly at this moment, a great favourite of mine, that I noticed out of the side of my bulging eye, a small thing hopping across the floor. My floor. A small dark thing a hip-hop-hopping. But it was OK, just a baby frog, come in from the garden, desperate to get outside again. It took skill and patience to coax it onto a sheet of paper – it kept sliding off, heading away from the open door into a dark corner where I lost it for seconds at a time – while keeping attention fixed on the screen – the aliens exterminating Ben Kingsley, Ben Kingsley's resolute team destroying the aliens, Pre-Raphaelite babes and all – but I got it out safely and myself back into the chair for the climax – too much of a climax as usual, fire and water, hangings by the fingertips, hideous mouths agape and screaming (aliens) or pursed with pain and tension (human) – all that – until it's over, or so you think, as our heroes, exiting from the sewer, celebrate their survival, the survival of our world, all that, until the camera has a second thought, nips back to observe a rat eyeing another rat – its tongue shoots out, wraps itself around the other rat, hauls it in. *Vivat!* So really it was in rather an admiring and satisfied condition, the Co-proxamol and the sleeper now pleasantly combining in my system, that I stepped out of my study onto the brick path outside my door, and felt something squelch under my foot.

SOME CONFUSIONS

I'm trying to give up smoking. I'm halfway there, having cut down from sixty to thirty. The unused time I suddenly find myself confronted with, I try to dream away.

Harold phoned us here in Suffolk to say goodbye, he was this day leaving London for Dorset, he will be in Dorset for the next three weeks. Then he will return to London. He is being accompanied both ways by his wife Antonia.

Why did I write the above – he didn't say it at all like that, he said it in a simple, low-voiced, anxious sort of way, fearful of the journey, the uprooting – illness and hospitals do that to you, make you so need to be at home that leaving it, even just for Dorset, seems dangerous, guiding you in imagination back to illness and hospitals.

It is cold and wet tonight, and yet there are mosquitoes. The English tropics is what we have in Suffolk in early August. Cold, wet, and mosquitoes. That is the weather I am under tonight. English weather. Mosquitoes in the cold, the wet. Nevertheless, it is important to affirm that I am sixty-five, not sixty-six. Why then did I begin these pages with an assertion that I am sixty-six? I know I did because I had to burrow through a drawer in which all the past yellow pads – the pads leading up to this pad – have been put. I was looking for a key – the spare key – to this study, thinking I had lost my proper key, and believing there was a spare one somewhere in my desk – a small fit of old man's panic, because I didn't need the key in the first place, as I never lock my door until we go back to London – it was just that I found myself looking for it, even though I didn't need it, and didn't even know that that was what I was going through my pockets looking for until I couldn't find it, and so began my search for the spare one, pulling out the pads to see if it was under them, and so catching the first sentence I wrote, which was an inaccurate statement about my age, which induced further panic, was I sixty-six, and not sixty-five, as I've assumed since my last birthday, except in that brief instant when I wrote the sentence, had I, in fact, written the truth and been living a lie ever since. I went over to Victoria's study, ran stumblingly through the rain to her study, which is exactly like mine but on the other side of the garden, and knocked on her door, pushed it open, and asked her to tell me whether I was sixty-five or sixty-six. 'You are sixty-five,' she said. 'Are you quite sure?' 'Yes. Quite sure.' I was prepared to leave it at that, as she's never wrong on these matters, but she asked me why. 'Why?' she asked, 'why?' 'Well,' I said. 'Well, there's a difference between being sixty-five and sixty-six –' but then I couldn't go on to say that I'd written it down wrong in the first sentence of these writings, because I haven't told her that I'm writing them, I suppose she thinks I'm hammering away at some play or other and as I never talk about what I'm working on – in which case, why do I feel that I'm keeping these writings a secret from her, if I never talk anyway? Well, the answer to that is quite obvious – my not talking about these writings is a very different sort of not talking than not talking about a piece of work, it's a concealment rather than a reticence – so when she asked me why I wanted to know whether I was sixty-five or sixty-six I couldn't really think of an answer, 'Oh nothing, not important, no particular reason, just wanted to clear it up, really.' 'But you're wet, you've got yourself wet.' 'Well, it seemed urgent for a moment – you see, I've lost my key, the key to my study, and then I couldn't find my spare, so I got into a bit of a state, and my age came up, in the course of all this, was I sixty-five or six, for some reason.' 'Well, you're sixty-five,' she said, 'and the spare key is on the counter in the kitchen, with the other spare keys, and I don't know where your other key is, but it's probably somewhere,' and she nodded politely at her computer. The other key was actually on my desk, sort of melded into it from having been there ever since I put it there when we first arrived, so not visible to any but the no-nonsense sort of eye that I now also bring to the first sentence on the first page of the first yellow pad, and now here is the sentence that threw me into such turbulence – 'So here I am, two hours into my sixty-sixth year –' which of course means that I am sixty-five, though it's a bloody stupid way of saying it – but it's a perfectly reasonable way of writing it, I just read it bloody stupidly when in a state about losing one key and not being able to find another when I didn't need either of them, as a matter of fact –

CHEZ MOI

Been back in London for a month now. Harold has returned to the world. First a soft, troubled vacancy he seemed to be – there and not there at our usual table in Chez Moi, occasionally touching a hand or an arm and trembling out a question about the state of one's life; then a week later a fuller creature, by no means vigorous, not completely alert, bloodless but kindly. And now, this evening, the man himself smaller than before the cancer, still frail, most of his hair back though some of it in different places – the eyes beginning to brighten, the voice to strengthen – so in a few weeks, next week even – but probably not at Chez Moi. It closes down next week. Or possibly the week after. Or perhaps next month. Anyway, although it is definitely closing, when it is closing is not yet definite, which gives us quite a number of opportunities for last dinners before we go on holiday. Colin did say, though, that he was sure they'd be closed before we got back in early September, he was pretty confident that the latest date mentioned by his solicitor, or their solicitor, or the estate agent, 26 August would turn out to be the final one, although it might not be, what a pity, he said, we wouldn't be here for it if it was. All this confusion is quite simply explained; the two owners, Colin and Ricky, partners in life as well as in business, decided a few months ago that the time had come to retire – they're both sixty-five – and to travel around the world in boats, stopping off at this country and that as the fancy takes them, and then settling down to do all the things that retired people do, although I suspect they're not yet clear as to what such things would be in their case, as for the last almost forty years or so they've worked in their restaurant, Colin as the most charming maître d' in London, Ricky as the chef, mainly invisible in the kitchen, with very short holidays twice a year, so they've had little chance to practise for retirement, or drum up any hobbies. They're very similar, Colin and Ricky, not only in appearance – short and slim, with roundish, rather bookish faces and large, innocent, slightly troubled eyes – actually like elderly schoolboy brothers, one good at history, the other at geography – or a pair of elves, perhaps, benevolent elves – but vocally too. If one phones up to reserve one's table, one really has no idea whether one is talking to Colin or Ricky, although one naturally presumes it's Colin, taking reservations being more a maître d's function than a chef's (I doubt if you'd ever find Colin in the kitchen, and Ricky ever above stairs during business hours – Ricky is intensely shy (geography) while Colin is extremely sociable (history)) – nevertheless it's often turned out, towards the very end of a conversation, that I've made my reservation with Ricky and not with Colin, the call being put through to the flat in which they live, above the restaurant. This confusion has always pleased me – heterosexual couples may come to resemble each other in all kinds of ways, clothing, gait, political opinions, reading tastes, but while they might also even imitate each other's speech patterns, accents, affectations, etc., they could never sound in pitch, timbre, exactly like each other – sisters can, brothers can, sons and fathers, mothers and daughters, gay partners – but never a man and his woman, a woman and her man – I'm alone, why do I bother to make this completely useless distinction, and what is the distinction between a man and his woman and a woman and her man? Well, clearly, in any specific case, it wouldn't be a useless distinction, might even be making a defining point by going for one instead of another – Elizabeth Taylor springs immediately to mind here, the film star, that is, not the distinguished lady novelist, now I believe dead and therefore irrelevant – irrelevant, I mean, to the point I'm making about men and their women as opposed to women and their men – one would say Elizabeth Taylor and her man because one would be unlikely to remember his name, at least since post-Burton, post-Todd, post-Burton (if it was that way around) – who remembers who, apart from Todd and Burton and Burton, was married, is currently married, to Elizabeth Taylor, so that's the way one would have to put it if one were considering having them around for a drink and a bite – 'What about Elizabeth Taylor and her man,' or more convincingly, 'What about Liz Taylor and her man, eh?' Now on the male front – who would be the equivalent on the male front? – Well, I suppose Prince Charles, Charles and his woman, although that may be because I can never remember her name, recently confusing it with the name of a woman who got thrown off an island on television, because she wasn't a big enough celebrity – both names double-barrelled, hence my confusion, and hence my readiness to settle for Charles and his woman, let's have Charles around for a drink and a bite, etc., oh, and his woman too, of course, or possibly, and that woman of his too, of course.

Anyway, there are Colin and Ricky, the upstairs and downstairs of Chez Moi, fraternal partners in business and life, not only lookalikes but soundalikes, now having reached the age of sixty-five and deciding to retire themselves onto boats and cruises, with a view to settling down eventually. They can't sell the restaurant as a restaurant, the property being both small and extremely expensive. When they bought it forty years ago it was cheap, Holland Park not being the top address it's since become, and as they lived in the flat above and were prepared not to pay themselves on poor weeks, they could get along, if not always comfortably, then always safely. A restaurateur buying it now would have to fork out more than a million for the property, and given the shortage of table space, couldn't hope to recover his initial outlay – a hopeless business proposition, then, unless a multimillionaire steps forward whose idea of a charitable enterprise is to maintain a small restaurant for the benefit of Victoria and myself, who have come to think of it as our dining room, really, without the inconveniences of clearing up after ourselves –

– in short Colin and Ricky have had to put it on the market as a property destined for conversion into either a family residence or a couple of flats, which is why there have been so many last dinners, as deal after deal has fallen through, some speculators clearly attempting to sell the place before they'd bought it, others going in for reverse gazumping, i.e. lowering their offer once it'd been accepted, and then lowering it again once the lower offer has been accepted – and so one deadline after another has been passed, each new deadline the date for a last dinner at our usual table for four – I can't work out now for how many years Harold, Antonia, Victoria and I have dined at this table, in sickness and in health – and then there's the other table, the table for two, where Victoria and I have spent some of our brightest and certainly our darkest hours, my every birthday since we started together and it was crossing the road on our way to that table that I proposed, and it was also at that table that I sat with Alan Bates, my very last glass of champagne in front of me as I began to slip towards a coma – Alan supporting me past the table at which Antonia and Harold were sitting, my returning their anxious gaze with what was meant to be a cavalier salute, and it was there, at that table, that Harold and I discussed his directing a number of my plays, several of which were to star Alan, and there that Ian Hamilton and I met for dinner every few weeks for years up to the last week of his life and it was at that table –

COURTSHIP AND WEDDING

Chez Moi opened some forty years ago, three years before Victoria moved into this house. Occasionally she would cross the road for dinner, and soon became good friends with the two owners, Colin, the maître d', and Ricky, the chef. Ten years later, when Victoria and I started our affair, we would occasionally have lunch there. I hated it, thinking there to be a cold and protective glitter in the eye of the maître d', as it travelled between his infant neighbour and my middle-aged self, and no doubt it was my sense of his unseemly suspicions that caused me to behave offensively, grunting out my orders for more wine as I shoved my plate away, food untouched, and visibly, coarsely, failed to keep my hands to myself – indeed allowed them to travel all over his infant neighbour – well, not in fact, but every smile and sentence suggested that my hands would shortly close about the softly swelling etc. of my prey, who sat, as was (still is) her wont, with the air of a well-mannered fawn, though in possession of softly swelling etc., and an expression in her own eye that would have startled the maître d' if he'd glimpsed it, or if glimpsed, understood it. I suppose Philippe was around in those days, or perhaps he came shortly after – he's only recently turned thirty, which would mean that he was – Christ, in his late teens, at the most early twenties, when he arrived – my astonishment at working this out comes really from being unable to think of Philippe as ever having been anything but a fully formed assistant maître d', with his grown-up spectacles, his darkish-grey hair slicked back in the manner of my father's generation, and his air of experienced efficiency – his English is agreeably French, almost as if he'd practised to get the right professional accent – how could such a chap be anything but forty-three for the whole of his life? – though he has a tendency to puppyish weight changes, going from trim to portly and back again in a matter of weeks – perhaps he pads and unpads himself, experimenting with his size as he searches for the perfect embodiment of streamlined gravitas – anyway, in his varying shapes and constant effect he was certainly around during all the nights that I now remember, the humdrum nights, the jolly nights, the many nights when Harold raised his voice and silenced the rest of the restaurant with his political passions, the nights when Harold sat silent, humbled by his tumour, picking with feeble purpose at his food – and of course he was there for our wedding reception, over which he and Colin presided with the delicacy and warmth of – well, they looked like a pair of undertakers, actually, in their dark suits at three in the afternoon, such a sunny afternoon, a blessed and sunny afternoon, with all the details quite perfect – the confetti on my shoulders masking the dandruff, my toxic gait easily confused with a bridegroom's airborne strut – besides all attention was naturally focused on the bride, so light and graceful that she really did seem to be floating beside me, though in fact she was both guiding me with her free hand clamped around my elbow – the other clutching a bouquet – and keeping me upright by pressing the side of her body against the side of mine. Harold gave a great speech, which was interrupted only by himself when he shouted at a couple of special-occasion waiters, young and Italian to keep quiet! For God's sake! he was trying to make a bloody speech here! – so there was Harold's speech, it was our wedding, but somehow it lingers in the memory as Philippe's and Colin's event, and Ricky's too, of course, invisible in the kitchen but preparing the dishes to perfection, and sending them up at the perfect moment.

On the other hand, I was very drunk, and can't even remember whether we took George with us. We often take George, who feels perfectly chez elle under the table, asleep, probably dreaming of scraps falling onto her snout – which in fact they often do, from my plate – she seems able to shift them from snout to mouth without fully waking up, a toss of the head, a flutter of the eyelids, a dreamy swallow, a sigh, sleep again – a bit like the lady in Wallace Stevens's great poem, 'Sunday Morning', really, except George doesn't wear a peignoir. What is a peignoir, exactly?

It is midnight. We have to leave the house at 7 a.m. for Gatwick. Economic circumstances dictate Economy – first time since my twenties I've had to fly on the cheap. Perhaps if I'd done it when I could afford not to, but was physically up to it, I wouldn't have to do it now that I can't afford not to, but am physically frail, with a churning stomach and loosening but obdurate bowels. So memory poisons even the pleasures of the past – how I resent that young man strutting behind his porter to the Concorde check-in, resent him sprawling in his First Class armchair, hand wrapped around his glass of pre-flight champagne, most of all I resent him lurching off the plane in New York, so drunk that most of his forward movements carry him backwards, his liver and stomach-lining further eroded by the First Class liquids and solids, which right back then were contributing to the condition in which he finds himself decades on, as he contemplates the hurly-burly of democratic check-in, the cramped knees-up seat from which he will eye the lavatory that some swine will be occupying from the moment the seat-belt sign is off to the moment it flashes on again – enough, enough – at heart I am a merry man, I do believe. I'm taking a lot of books – particularly looking forward to Zola's *L'Assommoir*, which I've never read. The last Zola I read was *Nana*, a few years ago. Still remember my astonishment at the first chapter, the description of Nana's striptease, the tension in the theatre, the male audience's collective erection – never read anything like it, erotic, pornographic, obscene – a dangerous woman, a dangerous naked woman, a dangerous, naked public woman – I think my eyes popped, the front of my elderly trousers (all my trousers are at least twenty years old) stirred. God knows what would have happened if I'd come across *Nana* when I was sixteen – I'd have hurried myself back to the safe world of Hank Janson, where the women were decorously constrained, in private.

4

BACK IN THE SWIM

Yesterday, being the 15th, was the mid-August festival, the day I selected for us to travel on – not, of course, deliberately, but certainly stupidly, as I've been not only in Italy, but in this part of Italy, on the Ligurian coast, many times before, and know somewhere in my system what it's like – in fact, enough drifted into my consciousness for me to say to Victoria, 'Hey, let's go on the 15th, they all go home on the 15th, end of *vacanza* –' but of course the 15th is the day before the day they go home, in fact they turn up in large numbers, those who aren't already here, to celebrate being here for this one day at least – so walking around St Margarita looking for a chemist (I'd forgotten to pack toothbrush, paste, shaving equipment, etc.) in mid-afternoon was on the one hand like trekking around Leicester Square on New Year's Eve, pavements jammed, people shouting, laughing, lurching, and if Anglo-Saxon, vomiting, and on the other hand wasn't, because the sun was beating down. The chemists were closed, of course. Our hotel is on the curve of a steep hill, and looks, as you approach it, like a motel in an American movie – not the Bates Motel, which would have promised peace at last, but a motel in a sweltering and busy Midwest town, though set on the curve of a steep hill. One of my espadrilles, the one I put on my left foot, kept falling off. On the way back from the closed chemist Victoria and I, who scarcely ever quarrel, would have quarrelled, if we'd had the energy. The hotel beach is like the town's pavements, in that it's made of concrete, and almost as public in that, though it belongs to the hotel, it admits anyone who cares to pay a few euros. The sunbeds lie side by side, half an inch separating them, and the Italians are on them, and across them, and around them, and sometimes actually under them, and sometimes actually under each other on top of and underneath them – in other words behaving exactly as you expect Italians to behave on holiday. All this – this Hogarth in the sun, broiling and beating and bloody sun, hot, so hot that it's impossible to be in it, and the sea cold, so cold that it's impossible to be in that either – though, of course, that's where I mainly was, in the sea, or in a small pool of it contained by the slabs of concrete, being bumped and jostled by happy Italians, who really, I suspect, can't imagine being anywhere better – except back on the slabs of concrete, with their mobiles, their girlfriends, their boyfriends, their children, their parents, their grandparents, their grandchildren, their card games, their bottles and bottles of lotions – and of course so many of them look beautiful as well as happy, the sleekness and brownness and litheness of so many of them, from the middle-aged down to the toddlers, yes, sleek, lithe, brown toddlers, many of them completely naked, and the families touch, fondle, caress and stroke each other in a way that in England would bring around the social workers, and land them in courts and prisons – and there amongst them is a sixty-five-year-old Englishman, red of face, puffy and white of body, wearing tatterdemalion swimming trunks, his dead friend Ian's straw hat on his head, on his feet a pair of his dead brother's espadrilles, the left one of which keeps falling off – yes, there he was this afternoon, full of resentment and envy, wishing he was young, wishing he was Italian, and wishing above all that the water wasn't so cold. A cold Mediterranean, in the middle of

August! as I kept saying to Victoria, Christ! It's been a bad summer, she said; it's been in all the papers, hurricanes and floods everywhere – and returned to her book, a book apparently so good that nothing, neither the inferno in which she was reading it, nor my stimulating musings, could distract her from it.

It's three in the morning. The noise from the traffic on the road that runs not quite directly beneath us is beginning to thin out a little. There are some pedestrians, though, as I write this – young, Australian and drunk, who are discussing at the tops of their voices some of my early plays. I just checked up on Victoria, in the adjoining room. She is fast asleep. She looks small and forlorn without Errol at the foot, and George curled up against her spine or into her stomach, or spread in the most abandoned way on my side of the bed, on her back with her paws spread wide – another favourite position is on her side, front legs stretched forward, back legs stretched back, her ears flat against her head, as if she's flying – and perhaps she is, in her dreams – flying at speed and with purpose to a destination that will certainly have Victoria in it, and me too, if I'm lucky – but no George for Victoria tonight, no Errol, only me, and me not yet because here I am seated at the table on the small balcony, which to the right offers a view of the sea and the harbour of Santa Margarita, though to see it I have to lean far out over the edge of the balcony at an awkward, possibly fatal angle – 'he died looking for the sea' might be my epitaph, on the other hand they might think that I fell trying to peer through our neighbour's bedroom window. Our neighbour is, in fact, an old gentleman in his late eighties, from the look of him, with a wife a decade or so younger. They sit at the table next to us in the dining room, which, with its bright lighting, its rows of square white tables, and its large, shiny mirrors, resembles a restaurant in an English seaside hotel in the middle of the last century, the only difference being that it's packed, not with middle-class English families, stiff and silent, but with Italians of all ages, from two months to a hundred and two years, who enjoy everything from their own voices to the unusually (for Italy) disgusting food – and there this evening Victoria and I sat in a kind of gloomy wonder that we were here, in this restaurant, in this hotel, and there next to us was our neighbour, our double neighbour in that he's our sleeping neighbour and our eating neighbour. He raised a withered hand in trembling salute every time I caught his eye, emanating goodwill towards even this surly-looking Englishman some twenty or thirty years his junior, and listened with joyful attentiveness to his wife, who talked at him smilingly, but her voice has a rasp in it – perhaps he's deaf, reads her smile but doesn't hear her tone – anyway, charming though the old chap evidently is, and pleasant indeed to have him next door at dinner and next door in bed, tomorrow we start looking for another hotel – failing that a larger room with a direct view onto the sea, and failing that – failing that George will have to fly out to Santa Margarita, with Errol on her back, or between her paws. Or we'll fly back to her, possibly.

The Australians have gone, presumably to check on their texts. Now below there's just the traffic, sporadically, and above, here's me, on holiday.

A NEIGHBOURLY SALUTE

Last night, after dinner, we were sitting in the hotel lobby, trying to decide whether we had the energy to walk down the hill – no, we had the energy for that, but whether we would have enough to walk back up the hill after walking down it. Our fellow guests were playing bridge, or talking in large groups, small groups, lively and absorbed. Suddenly there was the wail of an ambulance, then a group of men and women in medical-type overalls, clutching bags and a stretcher, ran into the lobby, stopped briefly at the desk then ran, two or three of them, up the narrow staircase, while the other two or three of them squeezed into the small lift with the stretcher. Apart from cursory glances and mild exclamations nobody else in the lobby paid much attention. Victoria and I sat, though, as if something of importance depended on the next few minutes. The lift came down again, the two or three got out without the stretcher, waited. The others came down the staircase, manoeuvring with great skill the stretcher on which the old chap, our neighbour, was stretched – really, I don't know how they did it, managed to control the angle of the stretcher, get it around a sharp corner at the bottom without tumbling him off, and into the lobby, through which he was carried gently but with speed. His wife followed, talking at him with the same warm smile, slightly rasping tone. As they went past he raised his hand, as he'd done at the dinner table, in friendly salute, which, as once again nobody else was paying attention, I took for Victoria and myself, and raised my own hand, slightly shyly, to return it. Then they were through the door, we heard the ambulance start up, the whine of the siren. I went to the desk and asked the clerk, whether he was all right, the old gentleman. 'Oh, yes, yes,' he was busy over some papers, bills from the look of them, 'no problema,' which he translated for me as 'No problem.' Victoria and I sat on for a bit, then walked down the hill for coffee. We solved the problem of walking back up it by taking a taxi.

This morning, while we were being shown this room, or rather its large balcony, by the assistant manager, I said, 'The old gentleman, is he all right, then?' 'No,' he said, 'he did.' His English was pretty good, in fact this was about the only word he'd seriously mispronounced, if he'd mispronounced it, which he made clear he had, by confirming our suggested correction, 'Yes, yes, yes!' he said, irritated with himself, 'he die-ed. In the ambulance. Die-ed.' He said that the old chap had come to Santa Margarita every summer since childhood, it was the place he'd loved most in the world, had intended to be buried here, had picked out his spot years before. So that was that, then. Everything had gone to plan, no shipping of his body to Milan, Turin, wherever, just a neat transfer from a local hospital to a local graveyard via a local church. So we admired the view from the balcony, inspected this little area, not really a room when it comes to it, an attic, at the top of the rickety stairs, and agreed the terms, and here I am, writing it down. The old chap's death. The death of the old chap who yesterday evening sat at the next table, and last night – no, the night before – slept in the next room.

WHO WAS THAT YOUNG MAN?

This is the following night. The day was OK really, very hot but we've discovered that we can spend most of the day, from ten in the morning until seven in the evening, at the comfortable little bar just above the beach, which has shaded tables and an exceptionally nice pair of waiters, one, called Emilio, middle-aged, with a wry, melancholy face who speaks no English but seems to interpret our needs from our expressions, and Paolo, much younger, who has a shaven head, is slightly camp, and speaks good English. Paolo and Emilio guard our table whenever we pop down to the beach – I notice that I've taken to calling it a beach rather than a concrete slab – for a swim. We've also taken a beach cabin, where we can keep our swimming stuff, which we dry out on our beach-beds –

the only use to which they are put. So there at the table we sit, enjoying the bar life, the intensely intimate physicality of the families, the noisy flirting of the boys and girls, the toddlers toddling from group to group to receive caresses and licks on the cheeks and licks of ice cream, and if we look across from our tables we can see much the same scenes on the beach – oh, and there's no music, no music – so all the natural hurly-burly, laughter, shouting, occasional sobs from the children seem to harmonize with our reading, which we're mostly at, Victoria stuck deep into *Our Mutual Friend*, I in *L'Assommoir*, stuck deep in the winter slums of Paris –

We suddenly remembered that tonight was the last known last night of Chez Moi, surely the final one at last, so we decided to give Colin a ring, to say a final last goodbye, wish we were there (which we certainly did). Colin answered immediately, sounded immensely surprised to hear from Victoria, thought we were in Italy, and then immensely surprised to hear that we were, and then immensely surprised by her farewell speech – 'No, no,' he said, 'We'll be here after you get back. We're closing 9 September. Definitely. Well, almost definitely.' So Victoria booked a table for 9 September. She said Colin sounded cheerful; there were cheerful noises around him.

Then down to dinner. It was difficult. We're still at the same table, and the old chap's wife, now widow, is still at their old table, but in place of the old chap there is his son, daughter-in-law, their child, and a middle-aged man in a darkish suit that we think is probably the family lawyer, and they were doing a lot of rather emotional things, grieving, for instance, and reminiscing, and presumably going over funeral arrangements, some of this on their mobile phones – it was really a very concentrated family table, and we were seated so close that when the head waiter came over I wondered to him in a low voice if it wouldn't be more tactful to move us to another table, so that the bereft family wouldn't feel intruded on – now this head waiter is a rather distinguished-looking man, white hair and spectacles, and a round serious face – he looks like an academic, in fact, and has in fact the limited intelligence of an academic – his English isn't much good, although it sort of looks good – I mean, his face looks as if it speaks good English until you hear what he is saying. He also doesn't like to let on that he can't understand much of what you're saying – another characteristic of academics – the vanity of stupidity, or the stupidity of vanity – and so a real mess of a muttered conversation ensued, in which he kept glancing at the table of bereaved, who kept catching his glances, especially as he interpreted our concern for their privacy as complaints about the intrusiveness of their grief – getting everything the wrong way around, in other words, and attempting to reassure us that we would only have to put up with them for this one meal, they would be leaving in the morning after they'd finished their business, no, no, I said, we're the intruders – but it was hopeless, and we went through our meal (disgusting) with heads lowered in shame, and also to conceal our eruptions of laughter at the thought that we'd been understood to be complaining at having to sit at a table next to a family in grief – anyway, that's the end of that. We've decided we'll forfeit our pensions, and dine in the restaurants in town or up in the hills, so with luck we'll never have to see the head waiter again nor the five widows seated in a row against the wall, trembling soup, gravy and ice cream into their mouths, and out again in a couple of cases – perhaps they've all been coming to Santa Margarita since their girlhoods, have already chosen their last resting places, have children in Turin, Milan, waiting for the summons – but Victoria and I haven't been coming since our childhoods, haven't selected our graves, for us there'd be an awful muddle of coffins on planes, one of us mislaid, or hauled up into the wrong hold, heading for Trieste perhaps, while the other goes home to London. Such thoughts are not to be borne, up here in a little attic of the Hotel Metropole, Santa Margarita di Liguria.

And here's another thought not to be borne, that my present circumstances have turned me into a sort of poor relation to my younger self. A younger and vastly more preposterous – prosperous, I mean, of course, prosperous self, though there does also seem to be something preposterous about the man who first came to this part of Italy – the Ligurian coast – some thirty-five years ago. For one thing this man was comparatively rich. A play of his had just opened in London to considerable acclaim and a busy box office – 'The best thing I've ever done,' the producer informed me a few days after the first night, as we settled down to plan the leading man's replacement five months and three weeks before he would be needed on stage – but that's the way of it in the theatre with a success, you keep your nose to the grindstone (in the form of a trough, of course, Italian, called Luigi's, around the corner from the producer's office) so that your success is still there, playing to good houses, a year or two later – 'The best thing I've ever done,' he said, his eyes hooded – he's got a noble face, like a Roman conspirator's, 'that's what people are telling me. They've been phoning all day, telling me it's the best thing I've ever done.' He really did seem to believe that whoever had written it, directed it, was acting in it, he had not only produced it, he had produced it out of his sole self, in an act of something like parthenogenesis – but then the vanity of producers is far more disconcerting, in my experience, than the vanity of writers, directors, actors, because it's better disguised, manifesting itself only in an hour of extreme triumph, more usually it is cold, serpentine and negative – a matter of 'face' really, now I think about it, in fact it's suddenly perfectly clear to me that 'producer's face' is more accurate than 'producer's vanity', it's as particular to producers as athlete's foot is to athletes – no, the analogy doesn't hold, really, athlete's foot is an affliction that irritates and disgusts only the athlete him or herself, while producer's face is an affliction that irritates and disgusts other people, and most particularly the playwright, the directors, the actors. 'Face' has of course to be taken in the oriental (and old colonial) sense of dignity, self-importance, consciousness of the world's estimation – as in 'He decided that the only way he could save face was by flogging the little scamp in front of the assembled villagers' or 'What Yvonne refused to understand was that every time she visited Jamki in her tent, Gerald lost face with the Turks.' So forth. Face is why, unlike film producers, who dish out huge sums for the rights to novels, short stories, biographies, stage plays, television plays, often for no other purpose than to prevent some other film producer from buying them, theatre producers are reluctant to pay even small sums for the rights to a play, often managing to avoid putting down as much as a penny until the play is actually on the stage – the point being that if they do pay out even as little as a penny they feel that they are publicly committed to producing it, and failure to do so will mean losing 'face' with all the other producers in town, those colleagues and competitors who constitute their peer group. This is all a gross simplification, when I look at it, all I seem to be saying is that producers are pretty normal members of the human race, morally less developed than George, of course, so somewhere down here on a par with the likes of myself and really, I can't waste more time wrestling with their psychological complexities. Why did I get onto them, and where from – oh, yes, my being rich from my writing – no, not me, him, the man who first came to the Ligurian coast thirty years ago, who not only had a successful play, etc., he also had a job as a university lecturer for life, if he wanted it; he owned two houses outright, one in Highgate – well, just down from Highgate, across the Archway Road, in fact – and another in Devon; he had a pension plan, through his university job, and further pension plans from the proceeds of his writings – stage plays, television plays, film scripts – yes, that's how I see that youngish man now, in his prime, his pomp and his prime – he'd chosen the hotel from the Michelin guide, flipping urgently through its pages, noting only those categorized by two tall red towers, two squat red towers squashed between them, the grand hotels de luxe in other words, and pausing only at those right by the sea. Eventually his finger stopped at a hotel called Gran Hotel de due Castelli in Sestri Levante, down from Genoa, up from La Spezia. And so he came with his family to the Ligurian coast and the best hotel in the world, he truly believed – still believes – two castles, one containing the bedrooms, the other the restaurant, the two connected by two paths, one open, one sheltered against the rain – but when did it rain, in all the Sestri summers? Well, perhaps now and then, for an hour or two, to freshen up the great, shady lawns that sloped down towards the sea, or the pine woods that surround the two castles, or the myriads of paths that lead you by way of views of the town and its harbour to the lift that took you down through rock to a small bay, a natural swimming pool where childish swimmers swam, that opened into a larger bay where ordinary swimmers swam, that opened to the sea where proper swimmers swam. The tops of the rocks that surrounded these two bays were as flat as shelves, the gaps between them spanned by narrow bridges that swayed slightly, but only slightly alarmingly, because you felt as you crossed them that if they ever collapsed under you they would drop you into a warm and loving sea, from which benevolent hands would draw you out and lay you down in the sun to dry, and eventually you would find yourself settled at your usual table in the restaurant from which you could gaze out on the ships in the open sea, and the boats in Sestri harbour, and also watch out for the local train that spurted out of a tunnel in the mountain at 9.13 precisely every evening, would pause for a few moments, then with a faint husky roar shoot off into the tunnel opposite, its little lights, its little noise snuffling into the darkness – it was so friendly and mysterious this little train, so punctual, so clear in its duty, full of passengers we couldn't see going to places we knew, Chiavri, Lavagna, Cinque Terra, perhaps all the way to La Spezia – the pastries at the Due Castelli came from Genoa, by the way –

On our first night here I asked the head waiter whether his pastries too came from Genoa, I had to ask him several times before he understood, and when he did he laughed a proud, contemptuous, stupid laugh, 'We make it ourselves,' he said – of course they do, that's why most of it was still on my plate when we rose from the table –

– but when I think of that self in its prime, guzzling down the pastries from Genoa without adding an ounce or an inch, calling for another bottle of spumante, or French, let's have something French this time round! – watch him padding across the lawns to the lift, or diving off a rock with a cigarette in his mouth, I feel that I'm not just his poor relation, I'm his parent and his child, twice abandoned.

Well, where is he now? Hah! Look at him, look what's become of him! I wish he could see what's become of him – a chain-smoking, teetotal, alcoholic wreck scribbling away in the attic of the Hotel Metropole –

Or did he see me now, now and then, along with alternative

visions, and think, well, yes, could be, who knows? but in the meantime back to the spumante, actually it's better than the French, but it's cheaper, so I'll take the French, *che sera, sera* –

Now come on, it's rather pleasant up here in the attic, admit it, it's been a good day, quite a few swims, Victoria looks beautiful, healthy, turning brown, and my stomach is beginning to – well, no, but if I double the swimming, halve the chocolate which I only eat because the pastries are so vile –

Christ! I fell asleep during the above sentence, woke to the yellow pad jammed between my knees, right arm hanging down, pen dangling between my fingers, thank God it wasn't a cigarette. I do that more and more now, fall asleep with a lighted cigarette in my hand, the little sofa I'm sitting on is dry and musty, and the two chairs look like kindling – I could have burnt myself to a cinder, well then Victoria could have taken me home as hand-luggage, thus resolving the problem of my not having booked a spot in a graveyard in Santa Margarita – I'm not going to write any more in my yellow pad until we're away from this place, the Hotel Metropole in Santa Margarita, which neither of us likes, that I've brought us to, no, not until we're home again in London, and none of my memories has anything to do with my past.

BUNN

Here I am again, tonight, which is the night after last night, when I wrote that I wasn't going to do any more of this until we were back in London, but it occurs to me that if it's the truth I'm after, the truth of my life inasmuch as I understand it at this stage of my life, which of course I don't, because of course when you think about it, as soon as I've written a sentence I've already changed my life, or at least added to it, so that it's impossible ever to catch myself up into a state of completeness, to say here I am, that's all there is, now let's see what we've got – but even so there are certain matters that I've undertaken to face up to, however incompletely, and one of them is the financial side of things – and now is possibly the time to do that, when only ten miles and thirty-odd years separate me from those preposterously prosperous summers in Sestri Levante – how am I fallen! Woe and alack! But better put it as a question, if I'm to get on with it – How am I fallen? How come this woe and alack? Well, naturally, there are the usual reasons – extravagance, self-indulgence, fecklessness, etc., and there is a simple example of all three close to mind – every year after the fourth year of holidaying in Sestri Levante, I could no longer afford to do so, but did so, on the grounds that that's what we did every summer, which therefore made it an entitlement, its cost therefore an irrelevance.

Like Mr Micawber in *David Copperfield* I always assumed something would turn up, and it always did, right up until it didn't, and never did again.

And like David Copperfield, in *David Copperfield,* I was expert at the kind of hallucinatory economics that turned every snake into a ladder – whenever I dined in a fairly expensive restaurant, for instance, I calculated that I'd saved money by not dining in a very expensive one, and the money saved I tacked on to my inner bank account, as if it were money earned. Thus I became richer every time I ate out at my own expense, and twice as much richer when I ate out at someone else's expense. House champagne was a huge earner in the last days of my alcoholism, four bottles a day at a mere twelve quid a bottle, compared to the champagne I'd once drunk, Veuve Clicquot my favourite, at thirty-odd quid a bottle, so every time I put aside an empty bottle of house I was up another twenty-odd quid, courtesy of Veuve – calculations of this sort sustained me psychologically against all the portents, the chief of which were seemingly inexplicable surges of panic that were sometimes accompanied by little visions of humiliation, having my credit cards scissored, my cheques returned with insults, and then of larger visions, of a tramp-like figure roaming the streets, or sleeping in shop doorways – but I refused to read any of these visions literally, taking them as mere metaphors for my most fundamental terror, that I was going broke creatively, would be unable to finish another play. The waiters snipping credit cards and shopkeepers returning cheques were directors and producers rejecting my work. It was my talent that was turned away from theatres and television studios, was homeless, scrounging in doorways – rather like Faith in one of those poems by George Herbert, a personification and a lament, not a prediction.

And so they went on, these various forms of self-delusion, until the end, which came when my accountants drew my attention to an unpaid tax bill that had multiplied itself through fines on fines on fines until it had become almost unpayable, and every week that I failed to pay it because it was virtually unpayable it became more unpayable until it became actually and finally unpayable – 'But how did this happen?' I asked my accountant. 'Well,' he said, 'you see, it's gone on –' now what was the word he used, it made me think of mating, a sinister form of mating – 'accruing', yes, 'accruing', it had gone on 'accruing', my debt to the income tax. My accountant was a slow, thoughtful man – actually I assumed he was thoughtful because he was slow, but the truth might be that he was a slow, thoughtless man, after all he'd failed to notice that I owed the income tax all this money until it had accrued itself beyond the range even of hope, and had brought it to my attention

in a letter so pedestrian in its tone and so prolix in its details that
it took me two or three accruing weeks to grasp that my situation
had passed urgency, had passed emergency, had passed recovery,
and that I had no choice but to throw myself on the charity of
friends, whom I shall be repaying (gratefully, I need hardly say)
with a percentage of my royalties (those that are left to me) for the
rest of my life, and probably for a decade or two after it. This
accountant, the slow, thoughtless fellow, damaged me by – no,
that's not fair, let's try and be fair – let's say that there was collusion
between my negligence and his – my drunkenness and his – no,
let's not bother to be fair, let's not bother with him at all, really,
because the fatal damage was done long before the unpaid income
tax debacle, by the senior partners of the firm that he'd left, taking
me with him – yes, here's the thing, I went with him when he
decided to set up on his own because, precisely because, he was
slow and therefore seemed thoughtful, having lost hundreds of
thousands of pounds through the agency of his previous partners,
who were fast and fearless, full of cunning schemes and nifty
devices, whizz-kids, they were known to be, the whizz-kids of the
London entertainment industry. Senior whizz-kid was a small, drab
man, with pale cheeks and a long nose. His voice on the telephone,
which is where I usually met him, if a bit wispy was also wise and
kindly, the sort of voice you'd want in your ear if you were suddenly
in the dark, on a cliff's edge. Now he – let me call him Guppy, for
narrative purposes. Now Guppy's part in my economic downfall –
no, start with the other one, the junior whizz-kid – call him Bunn,
for narrative purposes – Bunn was a baggy sort of man, his suit
seemed to have more than the normal number of pockets and they
were always full, bulged, actually, but I never knew with what, and
his face – well, it didn't exactly bulge, but it was always a bit
swollen, as if he'd been beaten about the cheeks – perhaps by his

wife and children? Perhaps by Guppy? But he wasn't at all beaten in his manner, which was actually that of a beater, if not of a world-beater, he had a tendency to shout you down, even if you weren't actually speaking, and oh yes, he had astonishing eyebrows, twice as bushy as mine, which are really quite bushy, and slightly bogus-looking, his I mean, not mine, I was always surprised that they remained in place when he took off his spectacles to wipe his eyes, after he laughed – I had the greatest respect for Bunn, he was my idea of a bully, all right, but then he was bullying for me, and my then agent, who'd introduced me to both Guppy and Bunn, said that while Guppy was canny but conventional Bunn was famous for the flamboyance of his tax-avoiding schemes, he saved people thousands and thousands of pounds with one master-stroke, which in my case was to get me into containers. Containers, yes. The economy urgently needed containers, so that more goods could be moved more rapidly about the country, and between one country and another, from producer to consumer and no doubt back again – the government was prepared to make tax concessions to anyone who bought containers and leased them out – at least this was the situation as I understood it from Bunn, who made the enterprise seem so charmless that I knew it must be profitable.

In almost no time I found myself president or was it chairman? of a company that owned three containers, with Beryl my company secretary, and either Guppy or Bunn, I can't remember which, but probably Bunn, as the scheme was of his devising, the other member of my board. I did occasionally try to visualize them, my containers, packed with medical supplies, or dynamite, or nappies, hauled by trucks across frontiers, headlights in the rain, Yves Montand at the wheel, and there snared in his beams, naked under her raincoat, etc. – but what I could never properly visualize were the containers themselves – obviously they had wheels, but as for their shape, whether they were square, or oblong, or tube-shaped, or octagonal, whether they were decorated, had my name on them even – I really had no idea, and it never, of course, occurred to me to ask to have a look at them. Didn't occur to Bunn either, who was therefore outraged when he discovered that they didn't exist. 'You've been swindled!' he bellowed. 'Taken for a bloody ride!' 'But I've received cheques,' I said, 'made out to my company.' These cheques were for strangely inconsequential sums, twenty-seven pounds and six shillings sort of cheques – totally convincing therefore – 'Yes,' he said, infuriated by my naivety, 'of course they sent you cheques, that's how they pulled the wool over your eyes.' A waste of wool, really – as well as of money, as I wouldn't have noticed an absence of cheques, however consequential. 'And now of course you're in trouble with the income tax. As you didn't pay any tax on the containers, the money you spent on them is liable for tax, which will be backdated to the date of purchase, three and a half years ago.' This is the sort of meaning, if not the precise content, of what he said. 'But if they don't exist –' I said. 'Exactly the point. If your containers don't exist, you didn't spend the money on them, therefore the money you didn't spend is taxable,' etc. 'Plus fines accrued, of course.' Thus it was that I ended up paying tax (eighty-seven per cent) on money I no longer had, because it had been stolen from me. Tens of thousands of pounds stolen, tens of thousands of stolen pounds taxed – and in the days when tens of thousands meant something. Hah! It is raining cats and dogs here in Santa Margarita – I can hear them screaming.

Cats and dogs – dogs and cats – yes, I suspect that Victoria is now seriously, not just wistfully but intensely seriously missing George, Errol and Tom, dog, cat, cat, and would like to go home. Yes, we should go home, this really isn't a place we should have come to, but we flew Apex, and we can't change our tickets, we would have to buy completely new ones, and not even I can Copperfield that into a financial gain. But this has been a bad holiday, the only bad holiday we've ever had, together. Which makes us lucky, really, let's look at it that way – I've just been down to the balcony, stood just inside the sliding glass door, which I pulled open, stared out at sheets of lightning. I've heard the expression, read it often enough, assumed it was a *façon de parler*, but outside now, at rapid and regular intervals, great sheets, great white sheets of lightning blank out the darkness, and the thunder rolls, yes, it actually does, it rolls ahead of each sheet of lightning, like a proclamation. I went into the room, sat on the edge of the bed, looked at Victoria's face, turned upwards in sleep, found her hand under the covers, pressed it to let her know that I was there beside her, she was safe, come what may from the heavens. This is the last sentence I shall ever write in Santa Margarita, I swear it.

SOMETHING LIKE A SWAN

Well, it wasn't, because here's another one. I'm sitting at the beach café, having had my last swim – short and incisive, because the water's very cold again. Victoria's on one of the few beach-beds that haven't been packed away for next season, reading in the sun. Our taxi comes to take us to the airport in an hour, and already I have that odd feeling of regret – something Dr Johnson said about the pain of leaving a place you've become familiar with, even if you haven't been happy there – not that we've been unhappy, really, just ill-at-ease, at odds with it – but it looks calm and peaceful from where I'm sitting, the sea is shiny and I've just had a memory, which I want to write down, of somewhere else, a long time ago – a boy poised on the top of a high rock, the warm and welcoming

Mediterranean some thirty feet below. Running past him is a seemingly endless supply of children, many younger than he, bombing and diving into the water, fearless daredevils, free and easy, surging past him on either side, into the water, out, scampering up the rock and then past him again and again, and still he stands there, there he stands, posturing and posing his dive, arms out, feet clamped a little apart, legs slightly bowed – suddenly he drops his arms, scrambles down the rock, slithers and bumps himself into the sea, and takes off with speed and aplomb, becoming in the water strong and graceful, completely at ease, everything he isn't on dry land, where unfortunately he has to spend most of his time. I don't know who he is, or where he comes from in my memory – it can't be me, surely, I always jumped, didn't I? Or dived even, at that sort of age. Perhaps it's a metaphor for me as I am now, but it didn't come as a metaphor, it came as a memory, in an image, clear and distinct, not something lived through but something seen, seen yet also felt and endured, so who and why – here's Victoria, coming up the steps from the beach, her bag over her shoulder, book in hand. I've put Ian's hat on my head, and am now, quite positively, writing the last sentence I shall write in Santa Margarita.

GUPPY

It's 9 October, and we're just back from our last last dinner at Chez Moi, an affair which was dominated by George, who began the evening by barking another dog out of the restaurant – a lanky, greyhound sort of chap, callow and clumsy, virtually still a puppy, no match at all for George in terms of character, force of character – and ended it rolling about on a chair by the door, as the departing clientele stroked her stomach. I think Colin was relieved to find himself virtually usurped as the host, in fact it was probably his intention, as he'd encouraged George out from under our table and on to the chair, and when the men with their handshakes or the women with their embraces threatened to exceed what he could cope with, socially or emotionally, he swivelled them towards George, a mere foot or so away, as if a rub of her stomach was the final and proper formality. Of course everybody in the restaurant tonight was either from the neighbourhood, or old and faithful customers, and altogether it had a familiar feel to it, not familiar in its own context, London, W11, but familiar in experience, from those great French films of the thirties and forties – *Sous les Toits*, *Le Million*, etc. Victoria, George and I were the last to leave, walking back across the street about half an hour ago, and here I am, not really upset because I know in my heart that Chez Moi will open again tomorrow, and we might well decide to pop over for dinner – no, not tomorrow. Tomorrow's Sunday, and Chez Moi is closed on Sunday, on Sunday we go to Orsino's. Monday then. It'll certainly be open on Monday, whether we pop over or not.

But right now to the story of my finances, which I left unfinished in the little attic room in Santa Margarita di Liguria, on the night of the storm. I'd disposed of Bunn, I believe, but the thunder and lightning got between me and Guppy, who was more of an aristocrat when it came to losing my money – no sordid dabblings in the hurly-burly of the transport business for Guppy, it was a suit and a tie and a taxi to the famous Lloyd's building, where I shook hands with Guppyish sort of men, but more expensively dressed, had words I don't remember spoken at me before witnesses, and then signed at a specially laid table a document giving someone the right to take possession of all my worldly goods in the event of an event that would never come to pass – 'Does that mean that if things go wrong, some catastrophe – I'd be wiped out?' I asked Guppy in the taxi back. 'I'm glad you raised that,' said Guppy, 'because as your sponsor I'm legally obliged to confirm that you could be wiped out, yes. And I suppose I shouldn't add that it won't happen. But it won't, because it can't, thank God.' He laughed from a long way behind his rather long nose, a frail sound, reassuring. 'That's the beauty of it. Can't happen.' Well, just as don't care was made to care, can't happen was made to happen – probably Guppy's mistake was to thank God that it couldn't, thus alerting Him to an overlooked duty. My recollection of how Guppy broke the news is a bit muddled – I remember a voice wispy with grief, my failure to grasp the significance of certain key words in a sentence that went something like this – 'many of the names will be worse hit than you or me, far worse hit – there have been suicides – don't forget I was in the same syndicate as you, we're both names in the same syndicate' – 'hit', 'names', 'syndicate' – the vocabulary of a Mafia movie, really. Still, I grasped the basic fact – that people who'd put their money into Lloyd's were metaphorically in the same boat as the passengers on the *Titanic* – no, doesn't quite work, with the *Titanic* you either sank or were saved, with Lloyd's there was a third category, in which I was to be found – most of me was sunk (the tens of thousands that I hadn't put into containers) but a solid bit of me was saved – the house, which I gave to Beryl when we got divorced, and my copyrights, which I sold when the fatal tax-with-fines-accrued came in a couple of years ago. I have therefore nothing left in the way of worldly goods except my books, five Olympia typewriters, two computers, two television sets plus videos, two desks, two chairs, and my honour – for which so far no takers.

HOW DOES HE DO IT?

Well, I know – I didn't deal with the question of how it is I manage to dine out regularly, far more regularly than I dine in, go to theatres, take holidays even in places like Santa Margarita, let alone in Barbados (again this year, I hope), when I've explained not only that I'm broke, but exactly how it is – fecklessness, self-indulgence, extravagance + Guppy, Bunn, containers, Lloyd's – that I came to be broke. What is my secret? By what alchemy do I turn an overdraft into a Club Class lifestyle? The assumption, of course, made by for instance people who occasionally interview me is that whatever the calamities of the past, I still have a flourishing career as a playwright, with an income to match – before my last play, *Japes*, opened at the Haymarket, for instance, three separate interviewers informed me that I was a success. 'As a successful playwright,' one of them began one of his questions, 'don't you feel –' or was it 'think' – 'Don't you feel or think –' 'Think' what? 'Feel' what? – I can't remember – whereas the other two put it as a straight proposition, incontrovertible: 'You are a successful playwright and therefore –' and therefore what? Well, so many things would flow from my being a successful playwright, among them the things that seem to flow from my not being a successful playwright – i.e., restaurants, taxis, holidays, best seats at Covent Garden, etc. – which, of course, brings us back to the conundrum, because the fact is that I make almost no money from my plays, not even those from my golden past that are still sometimes politely referred to as 'classics', which of course they can't be, since one of the attributes of a classic is that it is frequently to be found on the stage. My classics exist mainly as points of reference in the memories of older theatre-goers – occasionally, I receive programmes of productions in Eastern Europe, Turkey, Japan,

Australia, then briefly I swell with the idea of myself as an international playwright, and try not to note that the theatres involved are of studio size, in towns I've never heard of and frequently can't pronounce, generating royalties that scarcely ever make it to three figures.

I really can't face listing all the areas in which I fail financially, a doleful business that also requires a head for the arithmetic of minus – let's look at the pluses – at how many tax-free years I've managed to win for myself, yes, win for myself, that's how to put it, and furthermore the fact remains – at least until further notice – that I get by, and in some comfort, possibly even with an appearance of dash – how do I do it? The solution is actually quite simple, but – but I can't bring myself to write it down quite yet. I'd prefer to write it down in darkness. Double darkness. There is still a greyish tinge to the sky, a sky no longer autumnal, but wintery, and it's only midday. Some time after midnight then, though not necessarily tonight, I'll put the words down.

I passed Chez Moi this evening, on my way to and from posting another useless letter to my bank. There is a proclamation in the window announcing that the restaurant has closed, regretting inconvenience to customers. On the pavement outside there are bags of rubbish, and an empty open box that was yesterday full of pepper mills, salt cellars, ashtrays, left there for passers-by to take. In our house, arranged around our kitchen table, are six of the chairs – the most comfortable chairs I've ever sat in in a restaurant; on the wall in our hall hangs a small painting of a young woman reading – the same painting, and therefore the same young woman, I trust, that used to hang above the table for two, our table, Victoria's and mine. A similar painting, of a young lady playing cards, that used to hang over the table for four, the table where the Grays sat with the Pinters and the Pinters with the Grays, hangs on a wall in

Antonia's and Harold's house. Within a week or so the builders will start work on converting Chez Moi into two little town houses.

Two forty-five a.m. Nice and dark. I've just been down to the kitchen to give Errol a plate of ham. Ditto Tom, who is getting frail with age. I had to lift her onto the counter. She eats on the counter because Errol steals her food if it's put on the floor. Odd this – Errol can leap onto the counter without much effort, but never does, even if Tom's bowl is full of food and she's out. Tom, on the other hand, will wander about meowing mechanically until she's lifted onto the counter, but will never steal Errol's food, even if his bowl is full and he's out. Both Tom and Errol will steal George's food, however, even if George is in the kitchen and watching them at it. I'm not sure, though, that 'steal' is the right word to use – perhaps the more neutral 'take' or simply 'eat' would be more appropriate, though in the days when Tom's food was put on the floor, Errol did in fact steal it – at least he looked as if he were stealing it, gobbling it down quickly and furtively, seeming somehow to keep his back to all parts of the room on which he nevertheless managed to keep his eye, and he didn't saunter away from the bowl with a lazy contentment, as he does when he's eaten his own or George's food, but scuttled off by a mazy route that took him underneath the chairs and the table to a spot behind the door in the scullery. There's a sentence in between the last one and this one. It explains how I live quite stylishly, without having any money. Now I've written them, the words, in blue on yellow. I can look at them and move on, cross them out and move on, or tear up the page, drop it into the bin, and move on – whatever, I shall be moving on.

5

A FIRST CLASS PASSENGER

I've tried explaining to Victoria that I'm ill, possibly very ill. She nods sympathetically, continues with the packing. I point out that George is climbing into the suitcase, hoping to be packed into it and taken with us, isn't it heart-breaking? – 'There, there, darling,' I croon to George, 'don't want us to go, course you don't, and we don't want to leave you, we truly don't' – Victoria packs implacably away, while I toy with the idea of destroying my passport – one of the advantages of being a smoker, you can set fire to things without effort, almost passively, while sitting down – like this: place the passport on the floor, to the side of your chair, light your cigarette, smoke for a while – quite a while, so as not to waste it – then let the arm drop, the eyelids droop, the fingers open, the cigarette fall – and come to think of it, you could actually burn your old passport instead of your new one, who would know the difference from the ashes? and if they turn out to be your ashes, owing to a slight miscalculation, you won't need a passport. There's a high wind, by the way. A very high wind, that means business. Think of bucking about over the Atlantic in a wind like that, darling!

Our flight is cancelled. Naturally, BA being BA we didn't find this out until we were pulling up at the airport, which was when Victoria finally got through to their flight information desk or whatever – we'd checked on the internet regularly throughout the morning. The only flight, I'll write that again, the only flight that didn't show up on the BA website as cancelled was ours – 'We can't be,' I kept saying, 'we can't be passengers on the only plane flying out of Heathrow – if we are we're probably the only passengers on the only plane' – and all through this, the checking on the web, the permanently engaged BA, the anxious conversations, and the drive out to Heathrow, the wind was howling, trees swaying – one cracked and fell against a house at the end of our street – and news bulletins on radio and television were warning people to stay in while reporting maimings and deaths across the country. So, as I say, we got to the airport just as someone in the BA office at last answered Victoria on her mobile, and around we turned, back we came to Holland Park, the winds subsiding.

We are in fact now on the plane, have been airborne for about forty minutes. As BA combined yesterday's passengers with today's, the plane is packed, perhaps overloaded – the take-off was distinctly sluggish, and one has the impression that the plane isn't actually flying, it's dragging itself along, simultaneously airborne and earth-bound. My first event at the Harbourfront Literary Festival, an on-stage interview or colloquy or some such, is scheduled to take place four hours after we land in Toronto, at 9 p.m. their time, 2 a.m. ours. If we'd left punctually we'd have had two hours to get from the airport to the hotel, check in, rest, settle nerves, find the theatre, prepare for the stage – as it left half an hour late, we'll only have an hour and a half in which to do all these things – oh, they've just announced that because of strong headwinds it's going to take forty minutes extra, thus cutting by another forty minutes the time between our arriving at the airport, and my appearing at the theatre.

Well, here I am, let me try and relax. But how can I relax? My seat's at the top end of the cabin, Victoria's is at the bottom end –

to get to her I have to go through the galley, turn down into her aisle, not by any means a free and easy little stroll, but a sidling-up, cramped and contorted affair, not too popular with the stewards and stewardesses, whom you have to squeeze between as they stand about snacking and chatting. You also step directly into them when you come out of the lavatory, as it is situated virtually within the galley. The seat itself is high-tech. It has a panel in the armrest with an illuminated diagram on it, and patches on the diagram that you press to make the seat adjust to the diagram's contours – but none of the diagram contours seem to conform to the contours of my body, I either lie with my stomach up and my legs down, or sit with my head thrust forward and knees up. Finally, after wasting half an hour sliding and tilting myself into a sequence of unnatural positions, I've settled for the seat upright, bolt upright, in fact, in the seat belt buckled for take-off and landing position –

I've become acutely conscious that this ghastly and complicated seat is pointed into the top right corner of the cabin, making me feel that I'm sitting in a sort of cupboard, the air in this corner is still, almost lifeless, and full of dust – I can actually see the motes hanging there before I draw them up through my mouth and nostrils and down into my lungs – I've been coughing and wheezing, wheezing and coughing since we left Heathrow. Now I will relax. Now I shall relax. Now I must relax. I picked up a thriller at the airport, to which I will now turn, in the hope that it will take me out of myself, and even better, out of this plane, which I have given up any pretence of piloting. Read.

In the first twenty pages a young woman, Californian, described as 'vibrant' and 'sunny', full of plans for a weekend with her boyfriend in a cabin by the lake, is plucked off the pavement, stuffed into the back of a van, driven to a building site where she is disembowelled, dismembered, etc. – there is a lot of meticulous medical detail, entrails 'shiny', bodily fluids 'viscous' – and then dumped in a dumpster. That's the prologue and it's printed in italics. I'll pass on all the stuff – four hundred and twenty-six pages – in normal print, stick to my yellow pad, where I can make things as safe as I want –

The young man in the seat across the aisle keeps giving me slightly irritable glances, no doubt he's identified me as a smoker, whose continuous coughing and wheezing, which is irritating the shit out of him, is therefore my own fault, I want to say the dust, the dust's to blame, but then he'll point out that he's not coughing or wheezing, is he – do I smoke by any chance? I think he's Canadian, he's scowling but it's rather a bland scowl – he's summoned the steward – small motherly looking chap – they're muttering together – ah! steward asked me in a motherly sort of way if there's anything he could do to help, a glass of water? I've got a glass of water, I coughed at him, but if he could get rid of the dust? Dust, is there dust? he asked, affecting dismay and slight disbelief, can't you see the motes? I asked, suppressing the famous biblical quotation with a wheeze, as it wasn't apt, really, or was too apt, the motes in the Bible being in thine (i.e. mine) eye, after all, and not in his, and therefore I would have to cast out thine (mine) own eye, not he his, which might suit him but wouldn't suit me or thee, anyway he's gone to answer somebody else's ping, and the young Canadian is adjusting his seat so that his head is turned away from me, and really there is nothing I can do about it, so concentrate . . . On what? Oh yes.

How to begin?

On an up note.

MUMMY'S FOOTBALL BOOTS

I was pretty good at sports – very good at cricket, very good at athletics (apparently my Under Fourteen and a Half Long Jump record, seventeen feet nine inches (or was it three – let's split the difference, say seventeen feet six inches) still stands). I was just fifteen when I opened the batting for the First Eleven, fifteen when I played centre forward for the First Eleven – which made me seem a bit of a phenomenon, particularly when you consider that very soon I'd be vying for top-spot as a school intellectual, but in fact at soccer I wasn't a phenomenon so much as a natural – I could do all the basic stuff – I could dribble reasonably, pass reasonably and run fast, very fast actually, which was of course crucial – but I was a natural, a natural centre forward, in that I had a knack for getting into the right place in front of goal at the last possible instant, I could feel where the ball was going to go quite a few kicks before it got there, and I also had an instinct for where the goalkeeper wasn't.

The one practical problem that ran through my soccer life was that I frequently had to wear stolen boots. My own, the ones I started with each term, were gone within a week, either lost or stolen by another boy whose boots had been lost or stolen by another boy, etc., which meant that somewhere in my House changing rooms I had to seek out another pair, which meant that another boy, discovering his boots lost or (as was the case) stolen (by me) would have to seek out another pair, which meant that at certain stages in the sequence I might be, for a game or two, in possession of my own boots again, but I doubt if I would have noticed, or if I had, have made any special effort to hang on to them. Many of these boots fitted comfortably enough to feet for which, when initially purchased, they were the wrong size – if they were too large, an extra pair of those thick woolly socks, or in extreme cases, two extra pairs, would make up the difference, and if too small then the excitement of the game would soon make the pain of crunched-up toes unnoticed until afterwards, when the liberated toes burnt, and the nails were black with congested blood. But by and large the system worked – I played my first match in the First Eleven in boots that weren't mine and scored three goals, and the next in a different pair and scored two goals, and got two in the next in yet another pair of boots, and the next match was to be against Eton, the match of the season, and though I was scared that I wasn't really up to it, I never gave a thought to my boots. Nor of course to Mummy, who, on my sixteenth birthday, a few days before the Eton match, with Eton in mind, gave me for my birthday present a brand-new pair of football boots. I'd never seen a pair like them. I've never seen a pair since, like them. Possibly they were the only pair ever put on the market, especially designed to appeal to a mother with grand ambitions for her soccer-playing son, along with a profound desire to subvert them, and him. It's hard to describe these hated creatures from so long ago, what was so wrong about them from the moment I saw them – they looked, for one thing, enormous, though actually they fitted my feet perfectly. Worse than that, although they fitted my feet perfectly, they felt enormous, as if I were wearing two pairs of boots, my proper boots inside an overall of boots – the visible toes actually curled back on themselves, and the backs went up far beyond the backs of my ankles – in fact, as they take shape in memory they seem like deep-sea diving boots designed for a gigantic pixie. 'Yes, I knew you'd be pleased!' Mummy said, as I gave her a big thank-you kiss and a quick cuddle, Father's eyes upon me (sixteen today, remember, on the brink of manhood). 'They're a special sort,' she said, 'so nobody will take them by mistake!' It would have been a mistake all right, and a pretty stupid one, to want to take those boots anywhere, especially on one's feet – which is where they were, on mine, when the Westminster First Eleven trotted from the changing pavilion to the soccer pitch – First Ten really, as the eleventh was labouring after them, a substantial gap seeming to open up between him and them.

Mummy was at the match, and so was Daddy, and so was most of the school, on an involuntary basis – in fact, almost everybody who was anybody in my life seemed to have turned up except me – not that I couldn't be seen, floundering in a lonely sort of way in roughly the same spot for the first half, and in a different spot for the second half – or anyway, facing the opposite direction – at least I hope I managed to turn around at half time. Well, that's what it felt like. In fact, I did manage to touch the ball, once when I kicked off – i.e. tapped the ball sideways a foot or so – to start the match, and then when I kicked off again, late in the second half, after Eton had scored. The match ended in a draw 1–1. Our goal was scored by a boy called Crook. When I joined my parents briefly after the match, Mummy gave me a smile of angry compassion, no doubt reflecting that she would have played far better herself (but not if she'd been made to wear her boots, *her* boots is how I thought of them), my father drew on his pipe, impassive. Then there were the two friends they'd brought along, a Mr and Mrs Lumsden – her first name was Betty, Betty Lumsden, a red-headed woman who always made me feel shy because she was so pretty, I only remember her name, Betty, because I used to prickle every time my parents bandied it about – well, there I stood, briefly, avoiding all eyes, particularly Mrs Lumsden's, and then off for the team tea with the boys from Eton, again avoiding all eyes. 'Didn't see much of the ball, eh, Gray,' the sports master, a small, sleek man called Lowcock, said while I was changing. 'No, sir,' I said, though he was wrong, and I was lying. I'd seen all of the ball all the time, every second of the game.

I was dropped for the next match, played a few games for the Second Eleven in Mummy's boots, which by now had become much noticed, so there was no chance of suddenly appearing in somebody else's boots without those being noticed – perhaps by the somebody who owned them – played a few games for the House, I think, before I stopped playing altogether. It wasn't difficult to get out of things like football in those days at Westminster – and I'd been an anomaly, anyway, a sporty type who posed as an intellectual. I don't think I was missed by the rest of the First Eleven, who probably suspected me of being an intellectual posing as a centre forward. They probably came to regard my goals in my early games as flukes – which they weren't. I was a natural.

Sometimes I wonder what would have become of me if I'd gone on as a footballer, a cricketer. Three of my best memories now, at sixty-five, come from that period of my life – a late cut off a high-speed ball not that far outside my off stump that went skidding to the boundary, a perfectly executed shot that was entirely reflex, I'd never done one before, not even practised it in the nets, it was a wondrous moment, the sensation of it, it tingles down my arms as I write. Then there was my sweep of a spinning ball delivered by Ian Peebles, who was playing for the Old Westminsters and was, I suppose, in his forties, possibly fifties, when he bowled to me but nevertheless, in his prime, had played for England. It was the impertinence of that sweep that stays with me, rather than the sweep itself – and the look he gave me, of loathing, that can still make me tremble with joy. The third memory is of a goal I scored from outside the penalty box – I can see the players moving towards me, the goalkeeper behind them, and the spot in the corner of the net to which I knew the ball would fly as I was in the very act of kicking it. I had other moments too, that I can sum up by an act of will, but none that are alive in my body as those three, none that bring me such pleasure in myself for having been that self, to which I am still connected. Yes, that's it – that when I remember those moments I'm the same S. Gray then and now – the fifteen-year-old and the sixty-five-year-old fuse into a whole creature unseparated by time or crimes. The only other moments that bring me together in that way are moments of embarrassment and failure, that I struggle to forget when they try (why do they?) to surface. A drab addendum to a happy thought. How typical. How typical, too, to blame Mummy and her boots for funking out of football – you funked out of cricket, too, funkwit, can't claim you were wearing Mummy's boots or gloves or box when you lowered yourself down from opening the batting for the First Eleven to the Second, then a few House matches and into the library, to spend those afternoons you used to spend on the cricket and football pitches. The great thing about posing as an intellectual is that it was safer – that's the crude nub of the matter, safer than exposing yourself to failure on the football and cricket pitches. In other words, let's face it, would I have been any more mobile if I'd worn a proper pair of somebody else's boots for the Eton match? Well, yes, more mobile and as a consequence less visible, I'd have seen to that – I'd have been everywhere the ball wasn't, arriving just too late in front of goal, too late to miss – so in that sense the boots were an appropriate justice, they mired me down, showed me up to everybody, Mummy, Father, Lumsden, Mr Lowcock, Mrs Lumsden, the rest of the Eleven as being never near anywhere that mattered, unwilling, unable, afraid, whereas without them I'd have got away with it, looked willing and able in an if-only sort of way, if only he'd got there a fraction of a second earlier he might have made contact, etc., pity – looking for chances, but not getting them – as opposed to not looking for chances, so as not to miss when getting them – yes, with other boots I'd have hidden successfully, with Mummy's boots I couldn't even try to hide –

It was the same with my brief spell opening the batting, really, although that was more complicated. I was OK against fast bowling, the faster the better, the more dangerous the better, because I had no time to think, merely to react – so in that respect I could again be called a natural, a natural opener, the defensive stroke completed perfectly thoughtlessly, and always the right stroke therefore – but with the first change and the slower ball, especially the slower, spinning ball, the confusions began, the instinctive became the conscious self, hesitating, entangled in choice, seeing the fielders, the spectators, the umpire's expression – all during the flight of the ball, which I would eventually spoon up for a catch – it amounted to suicide really, getting myself caught off a ball that, in the nets, I would have hammered casually and brutally – so I got by at the crease for the early overs, and that might just have been enough to keep me in the team, after all an opener who can see off the fastest bowling is a useful opener, even if he doesn't score many runs, but in the field –

In the field, in unimportant games, House matches etc., I took blinders. Blinders. Once, far out near the boundary, I pedalled backwards at high speed, and then jumped backwards, to take in my left hand a catch that – that – well, frankly, it was an impossible catch that I took, that I nevertheless knew I was going to take as the ball left the bat, a most powerfully struck six all the way until it smacked into my hand just as I knew it would – 'Oh, well caught!' they all shouted, the umpire, the other fielders, the batsman himself – 'Oh, what a catch, well caught –!' said Mr Lowcock, who was walking tidily along the side of the boundary – and it was shortly after that that he watched me score an implacable, not to say interminable thirty-six – again for the Colts, and entirely against fast bowlers – and so plucked me from the Colts and had me open for the First Eleven and told the captain to make sure I fielded on the boundary, where I was one of the best fielders he'd ever seen, I took blinders.

The first few matches were OK because the ball never came near me. It was holding itself back, it turned out, for the important match, the match after the match with the Old Westminsters, when I'd swept Ian Peebles, the ex-England spinner – now how do I explain this, having explained that I couldn't play spinners here I am sweeping Peebles who spun for England, 'insolently' – isn't that the word I used – swept him 'insolently' for four. Hence his glare. Hence my gloating. What is the point I am making? Oh yes, the point I am making is that I once had it in me to do it, if only once. But why only once – was it because I didn't want a repeat of the embarrassment that accompanied my gloating? Was I embarrassed because I gloated, or was I embarrassed because I swept the old bugger for four in the first place? Was the hubris in the sweep, or in the gloat? Well, whichever, in the next match came nemesis, in the shape of the ball that wouldn't leave me alone – all afternoon it tracked me, even when the batsman presented it with a straight and dignified bat it shot off it with science-defying force, scudded across the turf, underneath my groping hand across the boundary. Wherever I manoeuvred myself, it came at me, failing to reach me only once, when it towered above me, – stopped in mid-air, stopped, just stopped for ten minutes or so, while the bowler shouted, 'Catch it!' and the captain shouted, 'Yours, Gray,' – and I waited for it awhile, my hands cupped, then as it began to drop some yards behind me, I did my back-pedal, the same sizzling back-pedal that Mr Lowcock had observed at close quarters, well, the same as far as the movement of my feet was concerned, but opposite in that it carried me further and further away from the ball, which landed a few yards in front of where I'd started out, and therefore rather more than a few yards from where I ended up. If I had a weakness in my fielding, by the way, it was in my arm: I couldn't throw very far, or accurately, which was why the batsman, instead of being out, bowled Tuffins, caught Gray, added three runs to his score, courtesy of Gray's throw, which went a short distance, and sideways, before it finally made it to the wicket-keeper, via another fielder. 'What happened to you, Gray?' Mr Lowcock asked after tea, as I was padding up to bat, a question he asked again a few minutes later, when I returned from batting – they'd opened the bowling with a left-arm slow, just for the one over, because their fast bowler had had to go back to the pavilion to change his boots. But I've jumped, I've jumped, in fact I've missed my own point – the point about the catch that I didn't make wasn't that I miscalculated the ball's trajectory and therefore failed to get near it, it was that my feet carried me backwards away from it on purpose, if the sudden, intense operation of a cowardly instinct can be said to be 'on purpose'. In other words I ran backwards away from the ball in order not to drop the catch – a dropped catch being when the ball either passes through the hands, or bounces out of them – a ball that lands many yards away from one's hands hasn't been dropped, it's merely been missed. Brave men drop catches. Cowards miss them. That's my point. Yes. So down to the Second Eleven, a few games for the House, into the library.

And there you are. I've ended the story of Mummy's football boots somewhere that wasn't at all in my mind when I kept postponing the writing of it – I don't know what I had in mind, really, except to blame Mummy for my failure to sustain a career in First Eleven football – and now I see that I've exonerated her by in effect blaming myself, pinpointing a basic character flaw – and what a flaw – I do think certain questions about her intervention need to be asked, though. Not, actually, how come that she, of all people, so proud of my sporting achievements, provided me with the means of showing myself up as unworthy during the Eton match of all matches – and why she gave me football boots as a birthday present – nobody gives anybody footwear without having them try them on before purchase (except carpet slippers perhaps) – and she'd been an athlete at the very highest level, knew the importance of being at ease in one's footwear – what would she have done if her mother had handed her a brand-new pair of spikes on the eve of her Olympic or Commonwealth high jump, presumably she would have said something sensible yet kindly – e.g. 'Thank you, Mummy, I look forward to wearing them after I've broken them in a bit,' would have done perfectly – would have done perfectly for me, too, so why didn't I? – well, from fear of hurting her feelings, but what were her feelings, what feelings lay behind the giving of this preposterously, not to say fatally, ill-judged gift? Actually, I think I know. I think she'd been energetically lazy, had lazily succumbed to a series of energetic associations – Si's birthday, got to get him something, left it late, late, well, here I am in Peter Jones (she was in Peter Jones every other afternoon, it was her favourite shop for being in, even when she had no money), trying on shoes for herself, shoes, Si, football, Eton, boots, boots yes, boots! – excuse me, I want a pair of football boots for my son, he's playing for his school First Eleven, Westminster, you know, against Eton, needs a new pair of boots, not too expensive, size eight, what would you recommend. Westminster. Against Eton, you see.' 'These, madam, I recommend these! Only pair left in size eight, it's by far and away the best boot of its kind on the market, especially for Westminster against Eton, nothing else like it, and going at a discount.' 'Taken. Taken and done!' cries Mummy. 'And at a discount too!' she would say later to James, because, quite simply, that was her way with presents, first priority – take no trouble; second priority, cheap as possible; third priority, please wrap it for me; and at the bottom of the list, if under consideration at all, actual suitability. And yet, as I've mentioned often enough, she had a generous spirit, our mother – but also a hasty, can't be bothered, slapdash spirit – and the carefulness with money was in fact against that spirit, a matter of necessity, she had so little at that time. If she'd had lots and lots, she'd have spent lots and lots, and the presents would have been lavishly inappropriate, instead of cheaply inappropriate.

That was the kind of rumination I'd had in mind, the treat I'd looked forward to serving up to myself when I'd got through all the unpleasant stuff – prostate and so forth, that kept putting me off putting it down, but now that I've finally put it down it strikes me that it wasn't a treat at all, that the rumination would go on to include the thought that the missed goals, the missed catches – most particularly the missed catches, because they were missed in comfortable boots – were pointers to the future – that throughout my life I have pedalled backwards, so to speak, away from opportunities that might have made the difference, from fear of messing them up – But what opportunities? Do opportunities of that sort happen with a life, hover in the air, waiting for a safe pair of hands to arrive under them, spill them, fail to arrive – are there moments like that with my children when I've failed to arrive? We're about to land in Toronto, Lester Pearson airport. So we've arrived.

No, we haven't. We're on the ground, but the captain's just informed us we can't get to our gate, it's blocked by a plane that should have taken off before we touched down. I'll be too late for the stage, another missed opportunity – but it won't be my fault, not my catch – my spirit is in place, hands cupped, it's the plane that's stationary, no, now actually shifting backwards, away from the gate.

ACCOMMODATING A SMOKER

I'm writing this in our Toronto hotel bedroom at three in the morning, sitting by the fractionally opened balcony door of our bedroom, trembling slightly with cold. Across the room, Victoria is in bed asleep – not a good sleep, she keeps stirring, coughing, because the smoke from my cigarette, which I keep trying to usher out through the crack in the door on to the balcony, is being blown back by the draught towards the bed. But then this has been what Harold would call 'a day and a half' – we had to wait twenty-five minutes to get to our gate, the plane that was blocking it had to unload a passenger who'd died as he was buckling on his safety belt – then it took another forty minutes for our bags to come through, so that we had just under half an hour to get to the theatre, no question of checking into the hotel first, etc. The young man sent by the Harbourfront Festival to pick us up had a slightly reckless appearance – he had sideboards, a jut of black beard, and fiery brown eyes – but was completely Canadian in style, relaxed and affable, as he assured us he'd get me on to the stage with time to spare, and he did, to the wings anyway, where I had a good three minutes in which to greet the Harbourfront director, the small, balding, squat and jovial Greg Gatenby, and the man who was going to do the interview, a man of imposing presence, tall, heavily built, with a short but somehow flowing grey beard and shrewdly twinkling eyes – gravitas, age, weight, dignity, decorum, fashion – he had the lot, and whatever our actual age difference, he was older than me in ways that matter in the world by a generation or two. His name was Michael Bradshaw, would doubtless have been Sir Michael Bradshaw if he'd stayed in his native England, was the director of Canadian Opera, and had especially asked to conduct this interview as he'd been a student of mine, at Queen Mary College, the University of London, and so the actual age difference was about ten years in his favour, when you work it out, which I didn't at the time, Good God, we said, all those years we said, as we shook each other by the hand, cuffed each other on the shoulder, I pretending that I remembered the mere boy out of which this monument to maturity had sprouted, and then I hurried off for a pee, combed my locks, so much darker and more luxuriant, if less dignified than his, then hurried to the wings just as Victoria was leaving them for the auditorium, stood in a kind of trance with my ex-student as we were introduced by someone who spoke around my name for several minutes on the subject of tortured and imprisoned writers, referring frequently to a chair that was kept empty on stage to remind us of the current fate of one particular writer – we were to regard it as his chair, the more his for his not being here to sit on it – and then my ex-student led me on to the stage. My main fear was that I would somehow find myself sitting down on the specially preserved, symbolically charged empty chair, but in fact I didn't manage to locate any empty chair on stage, though I noted through the glare of the lighting, quite a few empty seats in the auditorium.

I remember almost nothing about the interview, what he asked me or how I answered, but there was steady laughter from the audience, though whether I raised it or merely caused it I have no idea. The director, Greg Gatenby, and the interviewer, my ex-student, (Sir) Michael Bradshaw, both seemed to think it had gone

OK, and Victoria was impressed by the fact that I was capable of speech, considering the circumstances of our arrival – it was three in the morning our time by the time we'd finished – although adding, 'But of course you're used to being up at this hour, you're just getting going, really.' I pointed out that at this hour I was used to being up on my own, in my study, getting going by myself, I had very little experience of company at such an hour, except when I was so angry I needed two of me, one to expostulate, the other to expostulate back. I then smoked a cigarette in a marked-off smoking cubicle, was led to a chair in the lobby, where a quarter of a dozen people waited with books for me to sign – one of them by the biographer Michael Holroyd, the rest by me. At a table a few yards from mine the novelist David Lodge, who had been simultaneously interviewed in an adjacent theatre, was faced by a queue that seemed to stretch right out of the lobby on to the pavement, and beyond that possibly all the way to the airport, where planes containing David Lodge fans were even now banking, or whatever it is they do when there are too many of them to come down, stacking, yes, in the air, stacking, were plane loads of David Lodge fans. I had the advantage of him, though, in being able to get away within minutes, and within a few more minutes Victoria and I were in the hotel, which is called the Harbour Castle. The name is technically accurate in that it's on the harbour, and like a castle has a tower, two in fact, so that if you drew a diagram it would look exactly like a diagram of the Due Castelli, for instance, in Sestri Levante, but there are no lawns, pine trees, ocean views, and the drive up to it takes you through a vast concrete tunnel into a forecourt which is really a parking lot, at the end of which is a wall of black glass, with revolving doors guarded by men in burgundy uniforms who tip their top hats at you as you get into or out of your cab. The lobby's only distinguishing feature is that you can't smoke in it, nor can you smoke in any of the several public rooms, nor at the very long bar that stretches across half the lobby, and at which nobody was drinking when we went by to our elevator – in fact, it had a generally under-used look to it, the stool tops fresh and shiny, as if buttocks only settle on them long enough for some foul soft drink to be gulped down, nothing about it suggested that authentic bar life flowed and ebbed there – affairs started, marriages ended, births drunk to, dead friends toasted –

STRUTTING IN THE GRAVEYARD

Toronto seems ugly but pleasant – the city ugly, but the people pleasant, which is better than the other way around (Paris) or neither (Athens), but we haven't looked at much of it, yet, and perhaps won't. Literary festivals are rather strange, really, writers performing – why do people want to see them – us? Actually, I don't think anyone but Greg Gattenby particularly wants to see me, and I suspect he only wants – wanted – to see me because he has a copy of every book I've had published, in every language I've been published in, and wanted me to sign them all. When he brought in his first armful, looking, with his short burly frame, bare and muscular arms, as if he should have been carrying them in a hod, I assumed that that was the lot, but back he came, again and again, armful after armful, into the little smoking hutch in the hospitality suite, and not only did I come across editions in languages I didn't recognize, I also came across a long-playing record of the sound-track of the film of *Butley*, a Caedmon record, that I didn't know existed. I don't suppose I'm a special favourite of Greg's – in fact, I have no grounds for believing that he's read a single one of my plays, diaries or novels – but he's a compulsive collector, and of course specializes in collecting the work of the writers he invites to the Harbourfront Festival – which actually makes the signing tiresome, because you can't just scrawl your signature, you have to add a special sentence or two – 'For Greg, with thanks and admiration, Simon. Harbourfront, Oct 30th, 2002' but with variations, to show that this isn't a mechanical process, you're keeping him before you, a living and changing human creature – as indeed he is – as you write. Of course it's possible that he actually likes writers. He certainly treats them very well. Honours them, in fact. Although he looks as if he bounces them.

I think the reading went off all right, but of course I don't know what they made of it, really – I did passages from *Enter a Fox*, a sort of ramble around my life – the only other time I've read myself out loud publicly (the same passages) was last year, in New York, at the Jewish Y, where the audience laughed quite a lot. But these Toronto people, probably not many of them Jewish or New Yorkers, seemed uneasy about laughing, as if not sure it was mannerly, or perhaps they didn't find any of it particularly funny, though I now and then heard a guarded, chuckly sound and a few modulated grunts – but the grunts may have come from my brother Nigel, who uses grunts to indicate either interest or a polite lack of it. He and his wife Barbara had chosen to sit at a table directly under the lectern, which raised my consciousness somewhat during those opening dodgy moments, as did the chap who'd introduced me at the interview, though he made an identical speech, with the same references to a significantly unoccupied chair, which again I couldn't locate. I assumed he'd gone from the scene once he'd spoken my name and gestured me out of the wings to the lectern at last, but after I'd got out a few trembly sentences about what I was going to read I caught him out of the side of my eye, a tall,

balding man with glinting spectacles, standing just below the dais
to my right, staring up at me, and then as I began to read there was
his hand, reaching up and groping towards my book, to pluck it
from my grasp, I assumed. I almost lost my thread, only realizing
it was the mike he was really after when I heard my voice boom and
then straighten out – but I managed to keep my eyes on the page,
just as well, as the lectern was poorly lit and it was quite hard to
make out the small Faber print. Once I got going I could hear my
voice developing a bit of a strut, which was probably OK until I got
to the passage about visiting Piers's grave, when I was almost jaunty,
I think, until I suddenly took notice of what I was reading, and
pulled myself down a bit, not all the way down into a 'palpable
design' sort of melancholy, my voice didn't quaver – at least I hoped
it didn't.

GOING HOME

We're staying with Nigel and Barbara for the night, out in Oakville.
Victoria and Barbara went off to bed early. Nigel and I sat talking
about our prospects, now mainly behind us, and our past, which
was laid out stiffly before us in photograph albums – we flicked
through them rapidly, not really seeing them properly, both
wanting to talk only a little about not very much. He was tired, and
I couldn't remember any of the questions about family matters that
I'd been saving up for this meeting. There was a moment though,
when we found ourselves staring down at a photograph taken in
the garden in Halifax, in the mid-fifties of the last century. I just
wrote down 'of the last century' for the sake of it, really, the thought
of my having been a very young man halfway through 'the last
century' is oddly exciting, connecting me to those people who

announced, halfway through the last century, that they came from the 'last part of the last century', meaning in their cases the century before the last, or to put it all in basic terms, from the nineteenth century – what am I trying to say - well, I'm tired, Nigel's gone to bed, and I'm sitting in their dining-room, with one of the albums before me opened still at the photograph we looked at together, trying to remember anything about the circumstances – I mean, there we all are, the family Gray in what I suppose was its prime, the mother in a white summer frock, sitting on the grass, the usual cigarette strangely absent; to her right pubescent Piers, hair cut Canada style, his stare oddly intense (myopia, but as yet unrecognized), directly behind the mother there stands the father, arms folded, relaxed and confident, a man in his fifties with a good job, his own house, seeming to grow out of the family around him as if he were a tree in a tub – Nigel to his left, on one knee, arms bent, smiling and urgent, like an American footballer, and to his right, myself, hair long, a lock of it falling over my left eye, Hitler-style – unlike the other males, who are in short-sleeved summer shirts, I am wearing a black blazer that is evidently too large for me – the sleeves of it come over my wrists to my knuckles – and a white scarf that seems at first glance to be attached to the blazer, like an external lining – it's as if I've come into the frame from a different continent in a different season – what on earth was I up to? Can I have been making some sinister statement, winter man among the summer folk, grim and bleak, a harbinger? – then why the sensual smile, lips plump and moist – though moist could be the sunlight. It's a black and white photograph, of course, so the family might have actually been a festival of colours, my jacket not black but purple, my scarf lemon, and – I wonder who took it, there is absolutely no sense of an invisible other behind the camera, as there usually is with old photographs, I can't imagine who would have been there, available – oh, Daddy took it, of course, he arranged us as he wanted us, left a space for himself back row centre, set the camera which was on a tripod, then ran to his space, we would all hold our expressions, until the whirr and click, and there we still are, in black and white on a summer's afternoon in Halifax, Nova Scotia, with expressions held for fifty years or so, so far – and here on the other hand are Nigel and I, the two who are still alive, in Nigel's house in Oakville, outside Toronto – he asleep by now, I hope, and I looking down at this photograph in sudden amazement as I write this and - well, nothing else really.

It's an hour later and I'm still here, smoking in a house that's unused to smokers, there are no ashtrays, I'm using a saucer – jumpy, I feel jumpy. The flight tomorrow – then London again, and here's Piers in another photograph, six months old in a garment that comes down over his toes – he's on my lap, I'm sitting in an armchair, my chin resting lightly on the top of his almost bald head, Nigel is sitting on the arm of the chair, one finger touching Piers's little ear – it's a wonderfully clear photograph, so fresh – perfectly posed, perfectly natural – it must have been taken by a professional –

And here's another of Nigel and me, in the garden in Hayling Island, not long back from Montreal, we've still got the haircuts, I'm eight I should think, Nigel nine therefore and – ah yes, it would be about the time we killed the rat. We came across it late one afternoon on the road by the beach – claws stretching out, head poked forward, belly bloated – it made noises, mutterings and sighs as it pulled itself along to where, did it know – I remember the tail, stuck out from its back like a pink tube. We poked at it from a distance with sticks, threw stones at it, got braver and kicked at it, scraping and scuffing it about so that its head wagged from side to side, and there were the teeth of course – I always think that

I find men with rat-teeth sympathetic and kindly, goofy-looking, although I suppose if they also had pink tails – anyway when the rat's teeth are in the mouth of a rat, and you think of the rat scampering up your leg under your trousers (short trousers, I see from the photo), its tail whipping and teeth delving – but when it was stiff and dead at last, and looked so pitiful, and we knew that there was nothing we could do to make it right, we couldn't just let it go, or put it back, we'd finished it, it's life was over with and it was our doing – a few years older and we'd probably have said, 'Well, it was dying anyway, had to put it out of its misery, it would have been cruel not to, etc.' – in fact, we'd have said it before we'd begun to do it, as well as after we'd done it, but we didn't say anything, we went home, I can't remember our ever having talked about it and – well, there we are now in the garden with our ears sticking out, and our Canadian haircuts, and Nigel's front teeth also sticking out – he must have been making a face, he never had trouble with his teeth, never had to wear braces, never sprouted a pink tail – I'll ask him in the morning whether he remembers killing the rat – no, I'll forget in the morning, what with the packing, the goodbyes – and look, here's another one of Nigel and me, Hayling Island again but before Montreal, I'm about three, so he's four and a bit, and we're both sitting on the back of a Great Dane, her name was Sarah – no, Sari – she used to trot us about the garden, sometimes out of the garden and down the road a way, and look – who is this?

Yes, who is this?

From top to bottom: Nigel Gray, Simon Gray (middle)
and Piers Gray in 1946